'[A] beguiling nature diary . . . far from a cliched book about escaping mean city streets for a rural idyll . . . Harrison maps her joyful engagement with the natural world in both places, showing that we must learn to see, and act to preserve, the beauty we have on our doorsteps, wherever we live.' Caroline Sanderson, *The Bookseller*, Editor's Choice

'*The Stubborn Light of Things* is charged with the nature that's on so many of our doorsteps . . . Harrison has an easy, conversational style that offers up these gems in a way that somehow matches their easy beauty . . . Harrison's a deeply friendly presence in the book . . . a gift of a guide, and a gift of a writer.' Katherine Venn, *Caught by the River*, Book of the Month

'If *The Stubborn Light of Things* was an object other than a book, it would be a wooden countryside gate, drifting open at the gentlest of touches to let you on to the path beyond . . . If you've never read nature writing before, or you have and you're not sure about it, or if you revel in it – then this book is for you. It's for your loved ones. It's for everyone.' *The Little Bookery Blog*

'Reading *The Stubborn Light of Things* is like stumbling headlong into a bath of joy.' *Bookmunch*

and ...
man and ... *Tim...*
shortlisted for the Costa ...
the Women's Prize for Fiction ...
the Wainwright Prize (*Rain*). She li...
setting for the hit podcast which acco...
also called *The Stubborn Light of Things*. ...
@M_Z_Harrison

Further praise for *The Stubborn Light of Things*:

'Readers of *The Times* will know of Melissa Harrison, who
has been writing a monthly Nature Notebook column in
the paper for six years. This collection of her pieces takes
her from South London to Suffolk, where she now lives,
and she proves an immensely comfortable companion in
both locations, whether singing the glories of the capital's b... ...with a

MELISSA HARRISON

The Stubborn Light of Things

A *Nature Diary*

faber

First published in the UK and USA in 2020
by Faber & Faber Limited
Bloomsbury House
74–77 Great Russell Street
London WC1B 3DA

This paperback edition published in the UK and USA in 2021

Typeset by Faber & Faber Limited
Printed and bound by CPI Group (UK) Ltd, Croydon, CR0 4YY

Illustrations by Joanna Lisowiec

A CIP record for this book
is available from the British Library

ISBN 978-0-57136-351-3

2 4 6 8 10 9 7 5 3 1

*For all the weekend explorers, urban observers,
hopeful gardeners, all-weather dog walkers,
garden bird lovers, city park sunbathers, the very
new to nature and the lifelong outdoor types*

CONTENTS

A NOTE ON THE TEXT

In assembling this collection I've used the original copy I submitted to *The Times* each month, rather than the printed version which sometimes had to be cut to fit around images, or altered to reflect newspaper house style. A few additions and alterations have been made for clarification, or to reflect events that might have occurred since publication.

I am indebted to David Higham Associates for permission to quote from Dorothy L. Sayers's *Address to the Association for Latin Teaching*, 1952; to HarperCollins US for permission to quote from Annie Dillard's essay collection *Teaching a Stone to Talk: Expeditions and Encounters*, 1982; and Weidenfeld & Nicolson/Orion Publishing Group for permission to quote from Oliver Rackham's *The History of the Countryside*, 1986. Lines from W. H. Auden's 'The Wanderer' on p. 187 are included courtesy of Curtis Brown, New York.

I'm enormously grateful to Mike Smith and Cliff Martin at *The Times* for the work they put in to Saturday's Nature Notebook column, and remain extremely proud to be published there alongside my fellow Notebookers Miriam Darlington, Jim Dixon, Matthew Oates and Jonathan Tulloch.

INTRODUCTION

There was an overgrown pond in the next village when I was a child, choked with shaggy bulrushes and silver with frost in January. I wrote about it one afternoon at primary school, in my English lesson, and my teacher, a kind, generous woman called Judith Jessett, kept me back after class to tell me it was good.

I was a bright child, but I didn't have enough confidence to be truly creative: what made me feel safe was getting things right – not taking risks. Yet her words that day meant more to me than any qualifications I later achieved, either at secondary school or university; I carried them with me through my twenties like a tiny flame, precious but insubstantial. *Mrs Jessett once said I was good at describing nature*. But what use could come of that?

I was in my early thirties before I realised that there were people whose job it was to write descriptively about ponds and meadows, birds and trees. Kathleen Jamie's *Findings* was the first modern nature writing I discovered, and then Roger Deakin's *Wildwood*; Robert Macfarlane and Esther Woolfson came next. And then the whole canon opened up to me like a magic box: Richard Mabey, Mark Cocker, Nan Shepherd, Kenneth Allsop, J. A. Baker, Clare Leighton, Ronald Blythe, John Stewart Collis, Edward Thomas,

Richard Jefferies, all the way back to the parson-naturalist Gilbert White. On and on it went, wonderfully, transformatively; and as I read I began to make connections with the books I'd adored as a child, like *The Country Diary of an Edwardian Lady*, *Animal Tracks and Signs* and *The AA Book of the British Countryside* – even the four seasonal Ladybird books, *What to Look For in* . . .

Yet I didn't think I would ever qualify as a nature writer; for one thing I lived in South London, and more importantly I wasn't enough of an expert to hold forth on plants or birds or ecology. Instead I wrote a novel set in a city, *Clay*, into which I crammed all the noticing and description and love of the natural world I could. I contributed short pieces to the wonderful Caught by the River website, and began to pick up work reviewing books such as Helen Macdonald's *H is for Hawk* and Esther Woolfson's *Field Notes From a Hidden City* in the broadsheets. Still, what I most wanted to do was write descriptive non-fiction about the natural world. But while my expertise was growing exponentially as more and more of my life shifted to focus on nature and the countryside, I still didn't think I was allowed.

When, late in the spring of 2014, *The Times* got in touch to invite me to be one of a new team writing the Saturday 'Nature Notebook', the call came out of the blue. It was an amazing opportunity – not just to do the work I felt most called to, but also to share my beliefs about the value of nature and our precarious relationship to it with a more traditional readership than I had previously been able to reach. So I said yes, and although in the early pieces I can hear myself trying to find my voice, before long I was channelling the seven-year-old who had gazed at an icy pond and then conjured it up for a favourite teacher in a Silvine exercise book at school. Since then my monthly columns have been an absolute joy to write, and the warm, supportive and thoughtful responses from *Times* readers have given the lie to the modern journalists' advice about never looking at the comments below the line.

But while my column has continued uninterrupted for six years now, my life during that period changed a great deal. In 2014, I was the author of one novel, *Clay*, and I lived with my husband and rescue dog, Scout, in a rented flat in Streatham: a slightly down-at-heel area of South London with no Tube station, and boasting Europe's longest high street. Today I am the author of three novels and a work of nature writing (*Rain: Four Walks in English Weather*), the editor of four seasonal anthologies, and the writer and presenter of a hit podcast; I live alone in a Suffolk village and have Scout to stay as much as I can. So much happened between and around the world described in the columns; seeing them collected together is a reminder both of the continuity of the natural world and of what it was like to live through a period of intense change.

There are simple stories you could tell about the trajectory of these changes, and none of them would be true. One would be to set the countryside above the city; to turn my move into a classic 'nature-starved Londoner makes new life in rural idyll' narrative. But my love of nature was gloriously nourished in the city, something that's eminently possible for any city-dweller willing to start looking and noticing – a process I describe in my column for December 2014. I still feel a huge amount of affection for Streatham's wide avenues of Edwardian semis, its spacious parks and multicultural communities, and the busy, vibrant life I led there.

I didn't choose the countryside over the city; I decided I needed both. When I moved to Suffolk I continued to stay in the Smoke for two weeks a month so that I could keep working at dance music magazine *Mixmag*, something I'd done since I was thirty-one. First staying with friends in Bethnal Green, then in London Fields and latterly at the Barbican, the contrast with rural life continues to be something I need.

Yet for a nature writer to find herself in a place like this is still an astonishing gift. For my first year in Suffolk I lived in a brick-and-timber labourer's cottage that looked out across a water meadow where rabbits fed, hares boxed, egrets stalked the ditches and a barn owl quartered the long grass. After my landlord decided to move back in himself, I bought a place just a few miles away, a one-time one-up one-down built in 1701, set in a tiny village surrounded by arable fields. Farming around here isn't organic, and the hedges are in a bad state (as they are almost everywhere); but the small field sizes, plenty of woods and copses (important for pheasant shooting) and mixed, rotational cropping mean that while it's far from a rosy picture, there's more wildlife here than in the open, prairie-style agribusiness of the East Anglian peatlands, or the denuded uplands like Dartmoor and the Lake District – the bleak, unforgiving landscapes I loved first, and still long for. Here, nightingales and nightjars still arrive to breed each April, turtle doves purr on the village power cables, you can still find glow-worms and ruby-red corn poppies, and linnets and yellowhammers sing from the hedgerows in spring.

It was to share these riches that I began making the *Stubborn Light of Things* podcast in April 2020. With many of my urban friends enduring Covid-19 lockdown in gardenless flats, I wanted to make Suffolk's woods and fields available to as many people as possible, to help them keep in touch with the natural world and the changing seasons even if they couldn't go outdoors. With all the technical side taken care of by my brilliant friend the musician and producer Peter Rogers, and with the generous support of Faber, I began taking a field recorder out with me on my walks, capturing sounds from the dawn chorus to bell-ringing practice and describing the wildflowers, the weather and the crops in the fields. Each weekly episode included a poem, some entries from the Revd Gilbert White's diaries, one of my *Times* Nature Notebook columns and a guest appearance recorded often on just an ordinary smartphone and emailed in to me. The thousands of messages I received in support of the podcast were one of the things that got me through all those weeks living entirely alone. You can hear it at www.melissaharrison.co.uk/podcast.

I'm still writing my monthly *Times* column and enjoying it just as much as I did six years ago. It's a central strand of the connective tissue that runs through everything I make and do: the hope that I can engender a connection to the natural world that feels as rich and rewarding as it does to me – and which might even inspire readers to protect it in turn.

~ Melissa Harrison, November 2020

CITY

23 August 2014

The man from Lambeth Council has paid his twice-yearly visit with backpack and glyphosate spray gun, and now all the wildflowers on the pavements around my flat are browning and dying back.

It has to be done – or so I'm told – but I'll miss them nonetheless: Streatham's scruffy, litter-blown Zone 2 streets have been in modest bloom all summer, garden escapees like snapdragons, asters and lobelias competing for even the tiniest cracks with yellow corydalis, shepherd's purse, annual sowthistle and great willowherb. Some of the seeds, like the asters' airborne parachutes, will have blown in on the wind; others, like those of the shepherd's purse, may have arrived in birds' droppings. Some doubtless escaped from hanging baskets and window boxes and grew where they fell. A motley bunch, these 'outlaw plants' each found some tiny, unsanctioned purchase and quietly got on with growing and flowering, briefly greening the pavements and feeding bees, butterflies and other pollinators in the process.

It's a case of swings and roundabouts, though – or at least, central reservations, because around the corner from our flat, on Streatham High Road, Transport for London is trying to turn the ugly brick beds between the lanes into a long strip of wildflower meadow. For years they had been neglected, home only to litter, a few stunted ceanothus (Californian lilacs) and the odd clump of daffodils, but at the beginning of July these were removed and rolls of turf laid down in protective mesh, packed with young plants of fifty native and non-native species, including cowslips, meadow cranesbill, greater hawkbit, toadflax and yarrow. Spring, rather than high summer, might perhaps have been a better time to establish them, but so far most of the strips seem to be surviving, and hopefully they'll come into their own next spring. How well they do in the long term, given the need for regular watering and weeding, and the risk of nitrogen oxides and carbon compounds from traffic pollution over-enriching the soil, remains to be seen.

Streatham High Road is, according to a clearly erroneous 2002 poll, Britain's worst street – something that's doubtless at the back of the minds of those driving the recent campaign of beautification. Half a mile south of the wildflower experiment, a regiment of espalier lime trees has been planted between the busy lanes of the Red Route: trained on to what look like huge metal griddle pans, identical and evenly spaced, they look impossibly strange – hardly arboreal at all, but something else, sculpture perhaps – though they'll hopefully look a little better once they fill out. Sadly, a traffic accident did for five not long after they were planted; they have yet to be replaced.

*

Elsewhere the borough's trees are in fine fettle, fruiting wildly – albeit largely ignored. Not far from our flat a patch of pavement is covered in the purple skin, golden flesh and crunchy stones of the tiny sweet plums that have been raining down on it for a fortnight, unregarded; on my route to the bus stop pears dangle promiscuously over a tall fence, and on a nearby strip of waste ground a wilding apple – grown, I like to imagine, from a core thrown out of a passing car – will soon be ready to scrump.

On Tooting Common, where my husband and I walk our rescue dog, Scout, the tangles of blackberries are already in heavy fruit thanks to the recent mild winter, early spring and warm summer. A few people gather them, pushing circumspectly into the thickets with Tupperwares and sandwich bags, but mostly they rot on the briars. We have a damson tree in our garden and have already made crumble and five pots of jam; we spread out blankets, shake the trunk and another two kilos of fruit tumbles down, sticky, split and holding all the trapped sweetness of summer.

I miss the birds in August. I miss the dawn chorus – what we still have of it, given that an estimated 44 million British birds have been lost since 1966; I miss my local blackbird's ballsy evening performance from next door's gable; I miss the heart-stopping swifts screaming and dog-fighting above the streets. The breeding season is for the most part over; few, except the bellicose robin, will defend territories over winter, so there is now little cause to sing. And of course many songsters, like our local thrushes, are in moult.

Replacing an entire set of feathers takes energy and can even impede flight, making moulting birds vulnerable; it's hardly any wonder they keep quiet. In August, rustles from the undergrowth are often all I hear of my avian neighbours. Soon their ranks will be swelled by migratory birds overwintering here from Northern Europe – but not yet. August is a silent month.

27 September 2014

Two thirds of London's landscape is made up of gardens, parks, woods and water, making it one of the greenest major cities in Europe. It's a richly diverse wildlife habitat, with two national and one hundred local nature reserves, thirty-six Sites of Special Scientific Interest, more than twelve hundred Sites of Importance for Nature Conservation and several nationally important Biodiversity Action Plan areas, including acid and chalk grasslands, grazing marsh, heathlands and reed beds. It may seem surprising, but many parts of the capital are more wildlife-friendly than traditional farmland, where non-organic agriculture can create monocultures in which little else thrives. A fledgling campaign even aims to turn the city into the Greater London National Park, reimagining its sixteen hundred square kilometres as a vast working environment for both wildlife and people.*

One of London's most important contributions to biodiversity is its 3 million gardens, whose mixed borders, bird baths, compost heaps, lawns and hedges echo the 'ecotones' that are, all over the world, so rich in life: those areas between one type of habitat and the next, like the edges of woodlands and the margins of streams. Over three hundred species of bird have been recorded in the capital, and to them, gardens aren't the little kingdoms we experience them as, but long strips of green lying parallel to roads, with regular, useful fences to perch on and to act as windbreaks, plenty of cover for roosting and nesting, and lots of food: not just bird feeders, but seeds shed by the great assortment of plants we cultivate, and the caterpillars, greenfly and other invertebrates attracted by what we grow.

So to the city's busy, patchwork habitat now comes autumn, just as it does to the fields and farms: slowing the lawns' growth, stripping the trees and preparing plants for winter's long sleep. Blackbirds pick through the leaves rapidly accumulating on tired, dry lawns or cock their heads to listen for worms in the London clay, while red admirals and small tortoiseshell butterflies are beginning to seek out sheds and garages to winter in.

On our side of our road it is the north-facing back gardens that succumb to autumn first; the fronts of the houses

---

* London was officially declared the world's first National Park City on 22 July 2019.

get the sun, and many are still bright with late-season colour. While it may be far less pretty than the bought-in bedding plants that decorate our porch, the shaggy old ivy covering our shady back fence will feed late bees and shelter many birds through the coming colder nights.

Another sign of the new season is arachnids, as at this time of year they come into the open to seek a mate – sometimes venturing into our homes. This autumn is predicted to be a bumper one, as mild temperatures have led to an increase in the invertebrates spiders feed on and may well produce a spike in numbers. The Society of Biology has even launched an app, Spider In Da House, to help people identify and learn more about the twelve species most commonly found indoors – the idea being that with knowledge comes interest, and with interest comes a greater willingness to live alongside these fascinating creatures.

My bathroom is usually home to several slow-moving, long-legged *Pholcidae* whose only impact is the odd corner cobweb and the necessity for an occasional rescue from the shower; for the last fortnight it's also been home to first one *Tegenaria*, or house spider, and then a second. Larger, hairier and alarmingly fast, they have set up home behind my *Penguin English Journeys* series of books, and although they occasionally give me a start, I can't fault their taste.

It's the time of year when walking Scout begins to be problematic, as everywhere grey squirrels are down on the

ground and caching food, instead of up in the canopy, out of sight. Half Jack Russell and half Australian shepherd, Scout was a stray in rural Ireland for the first year of her life, and the hunting instinct – strong in terriers and terrier crosses – dies extremely hard.

Squirrels are astonishingly numerous across the capital; when my husband and I tried to switch the focus of Scout's obsession from squirrels to a squeaky ball using a method described in a book, we were unable to find a single green space to train her in that wasn't overrun. They scamper across roads and scurry up trees; they sit on garden walls and scold us as we pass, flicking their tails. The key to their success, and that of the other creatures that have learned to live alongside us, is adaptability: like rats, foxes and crows, these are intelligent animals that have learned to assess the risks, and the benefits, of human proximity. Squirrels have also learned some clever tricks – like only pretending to bury food when they think they're being watched, but actually hiding it elsewhere. As for what they're eating, I've found monkey nuts, an avocado stone and even a whole heel of bread buried in my planters. Who could help but admire that?

25 October 2014

The birds are on the move and it's exciting and unsettling in equal measure – as intimations of change often are. At night, now and again, I hear redwings calling overhead, and fieldfares have arrived in my local park from Scandinavia. Migrating birds tend to travel along 'flyways' – routes in the air that trace lines on land like rivers or even roads – and the sky over London has several; as a result, places like Parliament Hill, the Lea Valley and even Regent's Park can host big flocks of migrants as well as single rarities resting en route – and crowds of birders with binoculars and long lenses.

Following a few ornithological tweeters at this time of year populates your timeline with a real sense of seasonal excitement, whether it's huge, 4,500-strong flocks of wood pigeons passing over the Dartford Crossing, a short-eared owl arriving in Wanstead from Russia, or ring ouzels stopping off in Dagenham: there's a sudden feeling of influx, of adventure, of thousands of tiny feathered lives being trusted to the wind, the weather and our populous and sometimes hostile urban spaces. I would never have known that a migrating nightjar had stopped off on Middlesex Filter Beds on its way to winter in Senegal had I not seen first one, and then a cascade of incredulous tweets; it stayed for three nights in the end, resting on the same branch during the day in the species' characteristic elongated pose – despite a growing crowd – and setting out each evening at precisely 7.15 p.m. to hunt for moths.

With their huge black eyes, extraordinary camouflage, dramatic display flight and otherworldly, ventriloquial churr, it's hardly surprising that so much superstition has accumulated around these charismatic birds. Once known as fern-owls, nighthawks and goatsuckers, they were believed to steal animals' milk and cause distemper in calves; some even thought them to be the souls of unbaptised children. Of course, we know better these days, yet to find one in the hipster-driven borough of Hackney, albeit only for a few days, did feel almost supernatural – not a haunting, perhaps, but certainly a visitation from another, wilder world.

Migrating birds aren't the only incomers to London's cosmopolitan ecosystem; this week the writer and musician Ben Watt discovered a scorpion in his North London home. Trapped by his teenage daughter under a glass in her bedroom, it was taken to London Zoo, where the Head of Invertebrates identified it as a female *Euscorpius flavicaudis*, or European yellow-tailed scorpion. Rumours of breeding populations do crop up from time to time, with sightings everywhere from Ongar to Docklands, but it's thought that this one, common on the Continent, probably made its way to the city in a suitcase. With a rarely used and all but innocuous sting, these interesting invertebrates are no more of a threat to humans than the small population of non-native Aesculapian snakes that have established a colony in Camden Lock and which became the focus of some shamefully alarmist reporting earlier this year. Contrary to reports in the local press (and more widely), these non-venomous reptiles are not 'deadly', nor are they capable of 'taking out' dogs or babies; in fact, they subsist on rats and pigeons, something that many Londoners would doubtless consider a useful service. Sensibly, the London Invasive Species Initiative has no plans for a cull.

After dark, foxes are everywhere in London: silent shapes slipping across busy roads, weightlessly scaling six-foot walls or lingering in driveways like little *genii loci*. Sometimes they remain invisible, and my only clue to their presence is Scout, whose entire posture and gait changes, her usual casual trot suddenly soundless, spring-loaded and utterly engaged. Foxes fascinate her, and the feeling seems to be mutual: last year one would regularly follow us a few paces behind, a game of Grandmother's Footsteps that sometimes brought it right up to our gate, through which it would watch, wide-eyed, as I got out my keys and let us into the bright house. Currently there is another – very young, I think – that will sit, like a puppy, and call repeatedly to Scout, a quiet, inward yip accompanied by a head-bob that makes Scout freeze, and stare, and stare. What is being transmitted between them, I often wonder, in their congruous language of posture and tail position and ears? What arcane, mysterious information is being exchanged?

22 November 2014

We're getting a 'B-Line', apparently. It's not a new Tube line but part of the government's recently unveiled National Pollinator Strategy, a ten-year plan to protect

19

and support the UK's pollinating insects – not just bees, but flies, moths and even beetles – in recognition of both their economic and environmental value and their increasing vulnerability. Here in London, nine organisations have come together to create a corridor running from Enfield in the north to Croydon in the south, linking existing pollinator hotspots (or 'nectar points', as they're doubtless not allowed to call them) like nearby Brockwell Park. All along the B-Line, managers and owners of green spaces, from parks to gardens, will be encouraged to create pollen-rich habitats and manage them for wildlife – initially for five years, during which time insect numbers will be monitored, and hopefully beyond.

It can seem as though environmental groups are always coming up with new initiatives and plans – as well they might, if they are to respond effectively to new pressures on wildlife and new opportunities to protect it. But there are two things that make the London B-Line plan exciting to me. The first is the way it brings together several groups in order to achieve a clear common goal. The UK's conservation sector is fractured, with many organisations, from the large to the very specialist, having a shared stake in places and projects – but not always collaborating effectively, and often having to compete for scarce funds. So to see the London Wildlife Trust, the RSPB, Buglife, the Greater London Authority, Bee Collective and others teaming up is refreshing, a model for the kind of joined-up work that the environmental sector needs to do more of in future.

The other reason I like the B-Line project is that it's part of a slow sea change that's going on in the public understanding of nature. We're finally learning to think beyond what is either cheap, practical (for people) or merely decorative – and instead understand that our own priorities are just one of several things that need to be considered. For too long we've had a tendency to make decisions as though nothing counts but us humans; now, the cost of that short-sightedness is becoming clear.

Next year, when I walk around London's green spaces, I hope I'll see far less sterile summer bedding and insecticide spray being used, and far more unmown grass, native wildflowers – and weeds. Let the local letter-writers scribble their complaints to the council; the loss of our pollinators is a far greater concern than a few riotous parks and verges.

We've had our first frost – far later, no doubt, than everyone else. It was gone by morning; I wouldn't have known had I not taken Scout out just before bed and found it silently silvering the car windows on our street. So we brought in the spindly lemon tree that spends all summer soaking up the sun (and the traffic grime) on our porch. This year it produced three actual lemons – compared to none at all on our friends' far healthier-looking, but wholly outdoor-dwelling, Dorset specimens.

Frost is a signal plants respond to in different ways, from damage to dormancy; it can improve some crops, and 'blets' fruit like quinces and medlars, making them sweeter. A good frost was once valued for breaking up soil and killing pests and fungal spores; our fear of it, as modern gardeners, is partly due to our insistence on cultivating tender species from foreign parts, rather than those that have evolved to cope with our climate – like my poor long-suffering lemon tree.

It's the time of year when robins' song really starts to stand out – particularly as they're sensitive to artificial lighting and often sing at night in urban areas. Last Sunday my friend Peter, a DJ, returned from a gig at five in the morning, and rather than wake his sleeping household he wandered around south-west London for an hour or so as the dark sky slowly paled and a fingernail moon faded out. 'There were no cars, no trains running,' he told me; 'nobody about. But everywhere there were robins singing.' At last, he walked up the long road to his house as the street lights above him flickered off, one by one, the robins quietened, and a new day began.

27 December 2014

I grew up in leafy Surrey, the county with the highest concentration of trees in the UK. It wasn't the countryside, exactly; but it was very green, something I took entirely for granted. But when I moved to central London, seventeen years ago, I quickly became insulated from the seasons.

I lived at first in a flat above a garage in a treeless part of Zone 1, and worked in an air-conditioned office; rarely did I have a sense of the year's cycle except in terms of what to wear for each day's weather. And it sapped my joy in life until I felt empty and desolate, in need of something I didn't quite realise I had lost.

Finding my way back to nature took time. Moving a little further out and – eventually – to a flat with a little garden, adopting a dog and discovering green places to walk her helped; but I also had to change the way I looked at the city, and the things I let myself see. I needed to retune my eyes (and my other senses) to notice how much life there actually was around me, and to help me make imaginative relationships with the places I passed through each day.

Now I live a richly connected year, marked by seasonal events: the first snowdrop in my garden, cut and brought inside; the first blackbird's song listened out for, the first swift seen overhead; the first pocketful of glossy conkers brought home from the park, and the changing colours of my potted acer's bright leaves; the annual Perseid meteor shower, and Orion gradually clearing my neighbour's roof; the spring and autumn equinoxes; the shortest night, the shortest day.

And each December I pull up skeins of ivy from the garden and cut sprigs of holly to make a wreath for our door. I could go out and buy a much nicer (and neater) one, but to me there's a value in these rituals that runs deep. The city streets may be lit all night and our houses and offices warm; we can buy strawberries or asparagus at midwinter, if we want them, and carpet our pocket-square gardens in fake turf that never gets muddy and never dies. But there's a cost that comes with these privileges, these ingenious ways of disconnecting ourselves from natural cycles, and it is the loss of a great part of the richness of life.

Yet, invent what we may, the seasons still come to the city: the grass in the parks and verges sets seed, the swifts fly south and the year's midnight approaches and passes by. How much we see and feel of it all is in our hands.

Winter is great for enjoying goldfinches. They form busy 'charms' at this time of year and often occupy a whole tree or hedge, twittering 'like distant playgrounds', as the writer Paul Evans has said. Bright, enamelled jewels, they were once popular as captive birds; my father's copy of *British Birds in Their Haunts* by the Revd C. A. Johns, first published in 1862, says that, caged, they are 'known to tens of thousands of city folk who never heard the wild song of the Thrush, nor saw a Redbreast under any circumstances'. Happily, things have changed: not only is it illegal now to take birds from the wild, but robins and goldfinches have become common in cities too.

Once amber-listed, goldfinches came in at number seven in this year's Big Garden Birdwatch as more and more people put out nyger seed in special feeders, boosting their numbers and tempting them away from farmland where thistles, once their major food source, have proved no match for modern herbicides.

I love deciduous trees at this time of year. Leafless and stark, they seem more fully themselves; their branches form black traceries against the dull December skies, exposing their essential shape and structure and the way that each has grown: part nature, part circumstance. It is like character revealed.

Ash trees stand out, when their pennant leaves are down, for their large black trunks and drooping, beckoning twigs, while London planes are often pared back to pollarded fists. One oak on our nearby common leans in a way that's hard to make out when it's clothed in foliage; a rotting stump nearby suggests that it was shaded, while young, by a long-dead neighbour, and inclined sideways to reach the light.

When I am warm indoors, winter winds are revealed by the way the bare branches beyond my window sway silently against the sky. Stress builds lignin in a growing tree's fibres, strengthening them so that a wind-whipped tree will be tougher than its sheltered cousin; similarly a dry year, inscribed in a tree's heart, makes for slower growth and hard, dense wood. Each tree, then, is a record of difficulties faced and overcome: tempered, as we all are, by each passing year.

24 January 2015

Our view of what constitutes 'nature' is so partial, so skewed by everything from the Romantic poets to wildlife documentaries, landscape gardening to the heritage industry, that we often overlook what's on our own doorsteps, believing that nature is something grand and green that we have to get in the car to go and see. But the towns and cities that over 80 per cent of us live in are a habitat too; in fact, they can be a very rich one, teeming with clever and adaptable creatures that would reward our attention a thousand times over if only we didn't pass them by in search of a rural idyll.

Nowhere illustrates this more clearly than Oliver Road Lagoons, West Thurrock. Sandwiched between the Thames, the M25 and a huge Procter & Gamble factory, this utterly unprepossessing place once housed a huge post-war power station that pumped out tonnes of pulverised fuel ash, creating a weird lunar landscape. But when it closed in 1993, nature began to move in. The low-nutrient ash waste kept scrub from encroaching and allowed wildflowers to flourish. The compacted ash, warmed by the sun and undisturbed, became a haven for bugs, and before long the area was home to 1,300 types of invertebrates, birds and animals – including fifty endangered species, like the distinguished jumping spider found in only one other place in the entire UK. One lagoon was a Site of Special Scientific Interest due to its importance for overwintering waders and wildfowl, but dried out following the closure of the power station; when the northern part, a brownfield site, was targeted for development, Buglife stepped in to try to preserve it. Although the legal campaign was ultimately unsuccessful, the original development was abandoned and a less impactful scheme is being delivered, and last year the remaining parts of the site were given to the Land Trust, which will manage it in partnership with Buglife, securing its future for wildlife.

This month the process of rewetting the southern ashfield began. A tidal exchange system will ensure water levels rise and fall in step with the nearby Thames; it's hoped that wildfowl and waders will soon move back to the lagoon. A friend of mine is a recorder for the British Trust for Ornithology's Wetland Bird Survey and tells me he's counted 3,400 dunlin, 1,000 lapwings, 400 teal, 350 redshank, 300 black-tailed godwits, avocets, shelduck, snipe, jack snipe and curlews on the nearby marshes, as well as flocks of wintering finches: an astonishing avian congregation ready to join the rare spiders, carder bees and wildflowers in making use of this new site. It may not look like a picture postcard, but it's already a lot more rich, a lot more exciting, than some pretty green fields.

This month I put my name, along with twenty-seven other writers and conservationists, to a letter to the Oxford University Press, whose Junior Dictionary no longer includes words such as 'conker', 'starling' and 'brook', replacing them with 'celebrity', 'MP3 player' and 'blog'. It may seem at first glance a small matter, but a look at the full list of excisions, available online, makes for sobering reading; the vast preponderance are words to do with nature and the outdoors, gone in one seemingly very focused cull. Sir Andrew Motion, the former poet laureate, has said, 'By discarding so many country and landscape words from their Junior Dictionary, OUP deny children a store of words that is marvellous for its own sake, but also a vital means of connection and understanding. Their defence – that lots of children have no experience of the countryside – is ridiculous. Dictionaries exist to extend our knowledge, as much (or more) as they do to confirm what we already know or half-know.'

I agree; to delist these words is to make the very things they represent begin to disappear, because the process of putting words to things is how we come into relationship with them. As the writer Mark Cocker has said, 'Without language we will eventually lose the land itself.'

A witch hazel belonging to some friends of mine is in bloom. Its strange, spidery flowers, like red and yellow coral, or some kind of marine starfish, explode from the bare, woody stems like little party tricks: vegetal fireworks frozen in a shower of sparks, and far too exotic for this time of year. The fragrance is unusual: intense and spicy, and nothing like the astringent smell I associate with witch hazel preparations. The name derives from the Old English *wice*, meaning 'pliable', and its wood was once much prized for water divining. Looking at it now, in the January sunshine, it certainly does indicate spring – though of a seasonal, rather than watery, kind.

21 February 2015

This week I saw a red kite in South London. Not stuffed, or on a falconer's arm, or in the form of a toy: a real-life, wild-as-you-like, heart-stoppingly beautiful bird of prey with a wingspan wider than I am tall, wheeling over Tooting Common in the February sun as though nothing could be more normal, more everyday.

I was walking Scout; it had rained the night before and the grass was thick with mud, and I was watching the way it kicked up to spatter the white fur of her under-carriage and wondering if canine mudguards were worth inventing. She trotted ahead, five or six gulls taking off at her approach; I looked up to see them fly, and as I did so my eye was drawn past them, higher, to where a raptor rode thermals in wide, easy arcs. Only birds with broad wings – like buzzards, for example – can soar so beatlessly, but it still took me a moment to register what I was seeing because the context was so wrong. I stood and stared up, shielding my eyes, until my neck began to hurt; at last it circled lower, and I saw the underwing markings and unmistakable notched shape of the tail. A red kite! I found myself laughing out loud with the sheer astonishing gift of it, and looking around for someone, anyone, to tell.

London was thronged with kites right through the late medieval and Renaissance periods, when they scavenged rubbish and offal in the streets and at the dockyards. Persecuted as pests, and with fewer and fewer food sources in an ever-more sanitised city, by the mid-nineteenth century they were rare, both in London and across England – and by the end of the century they were extinct. My Tooting kite might have been a bird of passage from the Continent, or it could have commuted in from the M40 corridor, where there's now a healthy population thanks to a reintroduction programme that saw the first new pair breed in 1992. I stumbled on several at Runnymede in Surrey last year, where they were being mobbed by foul-mouthed parakeets; going by the geography, those ones were clearly of the Chilterns clan.

Red kites are spotted over central London a few times each year now, usually in late spring and early summer; five were seen together over Leyton in 2006. A pair have bred successfully in Hertfordshire, just outside the London boundary, so surely it won't be long before the city gets its first red kite chicks. As a South Londoner, my money's on Wimbledon Common, though Hampstead Heath is probably worth a flutter too.

As well as the big parks and commons, small patches of green space are vital in a city as crowded as London.

They're where the trees are that connect urbanites to the changing seasons; they house the birds whose songs commuters hear as they set out each morning; they're where parents take toddlers to introduce them to nature, and where city-dwellers can escape to, even for five minutes, without having to get in the car or on the train.

In my neighbouring borough of Southwark a small wood is under threat, and the campaign to save it is heartfelt and committed. Some dismiss such action as nimbyism, but to me it's inspiring: connecting with and defending our 'home patches' is a powerful way to protect the environment – more powerful, perhaps, than inciting guilt about far-off destruction that most of us feel, rightly or wrongly, we can't do much about. It will be useful to the locals' campaign if any rare or protected species can be found there, and of course the 'ecosystem services' of the trees will come into it; I wish, though, that the simple fact that people know and love Southwark Woods was enough.

Suddenly there are early crocuses everywhere: hosts of delicate lilac 'tommies' naturalised in graveyards, parks and gardens, their more robust, yolky cousins not far behind them. One roadside verge in Tottenham even has a long-established and much-studied colony of accidental hybrids: some white, some bicoloured or patterned, some with mixed blooms.

When crocuses open fully to the sun they make me think of baby birds' wide and importuning gapes: greedily, each clutch reaches skywards on delicate stems, top-heavy and hungry for light and life. Meanwhile, in the still bare trees above them, birds are beginning to pair up: great tits and blue tits are singing the shape of their new territories, and by the time the crocus's leaves have died back there'll be a new generation giving voice in our parks and gardens. Spring – as the crocus shouts – is nearly here.

21 *March* 2015

It's the time of year when frogspawn begins to appear, as if by magic, in ditches and lakes across the countryside – and in London too. Here, amphibians rely not only on places like the ponds at Hampstead Heath and Wimbledon Common to spawn, but also on urban back gardens – though the fashion for decking, and the boom in buy-to-let properties, means that fewer and fewer have ponds these days. With strong site fidelity, frogs and toads will continue returning to a garden long after any water has gone. I remember as a child visiting my much-loved aunt and uncle in Teddington and fishing dead frogs from their heated swimming pool, dug where a tiny kidney-shaped water feature had once been.

Spawn fascinates children in the same way that caterpillars and chrysalises do; partly, I think, because both are about transformation. The idea that a fully grown creature will emerge from such powerless and unpromising beginnings is hard to grasp, but exciting to contemplate – for it is something children are really trying to believe about themselves.

While you probably grew up, as I did, with relatively unfettered access to the natural world, that's harder to provide these days – and not just in cities. But a sea change is underway, as forward-thinking places like Greenwich Peninsula Ecology Park actively try to boost local engagement, the Forest School movement gains traction, and increasing numbers of children are now taken outside for at least some of their learning. London's schoolkids may not be able to play in the woods, unsupervised all day, as I did; but there's reason to hope that, if we can find a way to hold amphibian numbers steady, they'll grow up with their own memories of frogspawn and the sense of magic that it brings.

The nearest frogspawn to my house is in a tiny scrap of green a few streets away. Once the site of a large, long-demolished Victorian villa, when my husband and I moved to the area a decade ago it felt like a lost world: an unloved, overgrown tangle of trees, brambles and ivy in which one could just about detect the ghosts of a garden: a dank pond, an azalea, even a couple of redwoods among the scrub ash and sycamore. There was a gap in the fence, and people sometimes crept in there after it was locked up at night. Small fires were lit, and beer cans left; mattresses appeared and disappeared. But year after year, somebody kept feeding the birds. I was there often, fascinated by the

Victorian bottles, headless garden statues, roof tiles and other mysterious remnants that I'd find among the undergrowth, and as I poked about I kept coming across little sticks with coloured plastic ends. Eventually I discovered one suspended from a tree, stuck with seed, and realised they were bird food sticks – the kind you'd buy for a budgie. I never saw who hung them there.

My secret garden has been cleaned up and cut back now, and the fence mended. It boasts smart new benches, litter bins, woodchip paths and native planting – even an information board by the pond. It is prospected, safe, and known. That's undoubtedly a good thing, particularly for the local children who come to see the frogspawn – but I'm glad I knew it when the ivy still kept its secrets, and when somebody came to make their secret offerings to the birds.

Although feral pigeons can breed all year round, there's a clear increase in courtship behaviour at the moment, with much puffing, bowing and strutting taking place as spring temperatures slowly rise. Pigeons may not be high on many birders' lists, but I have no time for those who dismiss these clever and resourceful birds out of hand simply because of their ubiquity; after all, house sparrows were plentiful thirty years ago and are much missed now, and the passenger pigeon was possibly the most numerous bird in the world until we killed every single one of them within a generation. Far better, I think, to admire those few adaptable creatures, like pigeons, that somehow manage to live alongside us; better, too, to remind ourselves that when we call them 'flying rats' (or worse) it is simply projected disgust that we are expressing. It is, after all, our own waste, our own mess, that both rats and city pigeons survive on.

18 April 2015

At last, some proper spring sunshine. It only takes a day or two of warm weather before London's parks and gardens fill up with picnickers, tourists, Frisbee-throwers and office workers on their lunch breaks, and after what's felt like a long winter the sense of optimism and release has been palpable. How lucky we are in the capital to have so much green space to spill out into.

Smack-bang in the heart of the city, Hyde Park was packed to the gills with people when I visited with David Darrell-Lambert on a sunny weekday afternoon last week. An expert birder, and chair of the ornithological section of the London Natural History Society, David can pick out the note of a distant treecreeper over traffic, tourists and great tits in full song, and spot the tiny speck of a sparrowhawk in what looks to most of us like an empty sky. Soon it became clear that the park was just as busy with birds as it was with people – though had I been there alone I would only have picked out half the species we logged.

Most exciting, to me, was the little owl who glared briefly out at us from a crevice in a veteran oak, and the rare Cetti's warbler belting out a sudden song from a deep thicket in hopes of a mate. Like the parakeets that occasionally swung past us like viridian trapeze artists, both birds are immigrants to this country – though unlike the noisy and enterprising parakeets, neither is currently getting anyone's backs up.

The little owl, however, did undergo a period of being unfairly maligned when it first began to breed in Britain. Victorian gamekeepers, convinced quite wrongly that these foreign birds were damaging their livelihood by feasting on partridge and pheasant chicks (themselves, of course, non-natives, introduced to Britain for sport), were vocal in calling for little owls to be exterminated lest they spread uncontrollably across the country. It is to the great credit of the British Trust for Ornithology that this powerful lobby was resisted, in particular its researcher Alice Hibbert-Ware, who proved that their diet largely consisted of invertebrates and small mammals. Sadly, the UK's population of this charismatic little raptor is nevertheless in decline.

Cetti's warblers, meanwhile, are your classic LBJ ('little brown job'), and compound their unremarkable plumage with a habit of staying extremely well hidden; consequently, they're best identified by their strident song. Relatively common on the Continent, they first bred here in 1973 and now number a couple of thousand males. It's not thought that any commercial or leisure interests are being inconvenienced by their presence.

This week I found a seven-spot ladybird in my garden, newly emerged from hibernation: *Coccinella septempunctata*, 'the little seven-spotted red one'. With their rounded, glossy scarlet wing cases and beetling gait they look like tiny clockwork toys, and I can't help but smile whenever I see one. Yet ladybirds of all kinds can give you a real nip if handled – unlike parasitic wasps, which also work tirelessly to control aphids and other pests in our gardens, but are far less visually appealing. How capricious we can be in granting and withholding favour when it comes to the animal world; how easily we are won over by looks, or legend.

It is nearly hawthorn time, and the BBC's *Springwatch* programme is asking people to record their first sightings of its flowers as spring steals slowly north across our islands. 'May blowth' will dress London's roadsides and hedges just as it does in the countryside, weighing them down with clotted cream and filling the air with its ambiguous and unsettling perfume. In *Nature Near London*, written in 1883, Richard Jefferies notes its inextricable link to Englishness: 'You cannot pick up an old play, or book of the time when old English life was in the prime, without finding some reference to the hawthorn' – and it does seem to have accrued more legends than any of our other native species, including the oak. Long-lived, useful, and infused with century upon century of folklore, the hawthorn remains both tree and totem.

We've a long tradition in this country of phenology – recording the times of recurring natural phenomena, such as hawthorn blossom – starting with Robert Marsham's 'Indications of Spring', begun in 1736, and including the Royal Meteorological Society's network of recorders who published their results from 1891 until 1948; today, the Woodland Trust encourages people to record their seasonal observations on its website. These records help to build up a picture of how fast our climate is changing, and how plants and animals are being affected; the kind of year-round noticing they require is also a powerful way of creating a rich, lifelong connection with nature.

16 May 2015

As a nature lover, I feel so lucky to live in a city like London. Many of our most ambitious and forward-thinking conservation projects are taking place in urban areas, transforming heavily used landscapes, breaking ground with exciting new approaches – some of which can be harder to get off the ground in rural areas – and connecting appreciative and engaged residents with the natural world.

One such project is Woodberry Wetlands in the heart of East London. A construction scheme to build new homes – 41 per cent of which will be for social housing and shared ownership – is occurring in tandem with the transformation of a reservoir next to the building site into a wetland nature reserve managed by the London Wildlife Trust. Not only will the site be a haven for wildlife including frogs and newts, reed buntings, terns and reed warblers (all already present, despite the ongoing building work), it will also be invaluable for helping people in Stoke Newington connect to nature.

A drinking water reservoir was built here in 1833, its contents, until 1980, disinfected with chlorine and sodium phosphate gas. Once that stopped, the wildlife began to return, and it was designated a Site of Metropolitan Importance for Nature Conservation in 1987. Since 2010, London Wildlife Trust has been establishing reed beds and nesting islets, planting wildflowers, hedgerows and fruit trees, and converting the Grade II-listed coalhouse to a visitor centre and cafe; they've also recruited seventy local volunteers to help care for the site.

It's already clear what a special place it will be when it's open. To see the tower blocks of the East London skyline through the elegant, waving pennants of the phragmites reeds that already fringe the reservoir is a magically dissonant experience. The water level has been lowered so that silt rich in invertebrates can be dredged up and used to create reed bed islands where birds can nest, safe from foxes and cats. There will be boardwalks through the head-high reeds, a hide for birdwatchers and an education area for school groups. That much of this demanding work is being carried out with the help of volunteers is testament to the depth of local commitment to the site, which will not only provide a new home for London's wild inhabitants, but boost humans' health, happiness – and property prices too, no doubt.

On the way back from visiting my polling station I was astonished to see the unmistakable yellow flowers of oilseed rape at the base of a tree. Farmland escapees are common in the countryside, but this plant must have travelled some distance to make its home in the capital. I think the likeliest explanation is that a finch visited a rape field sometime last summer – perhaps in East Sussex or Kent – and feasted on fallen pods and spilled seeds. It then wintered in London, at some point perching in the tree and depositing some of the rapeseeds below: an avian form of guerrilla gardening.

Ever since reading Richard Mabey's book *Weeds: The Story of Outlaw Plants* I've been fascinated by the tactics plants employ to move around – their backstories, I suppose. Cities are full of botanical migrants, from gutter lobelias growing under pub window boxes to rogue tomato plants and rocket born from binned sandwiches. The buddleia that sprouts from railway sidings and downpipes came here from China; beloved of bees and butterflies, it's hard to imagine the city without it now.

Neither the left nor the right has a monopoly on caring about wildlife, but in the wake of last week's return to a Conservative majority many of my friends who work in conservation are worried about what the future might hold. Some fear the adoption of biodiversity offsetting (in which destruction of habitats such as ancient woodland is green-lit if restoration is carried out elsewhere), or are concerned about what the result of an EU referendum might mean for environmental legislation. Others are anxious about the future of Natural England and Defra, the badger cull, whether the ban on harmful neonicotinoids could be repealed, the introduction of GM crops, raptor persecution on grouse moors, HS2 and hunting. All hope that climate change – including fossil fuel use and renewables – is treated seriously and consistently.

There's also deep concern about a possible relaxation of planning laws – particularly as they affect Sites of Special Scientific Interest and greenbelt land. Lodge Hill in Kent is home to some of our last breeding nightingales, and is currently under threat – despite being Britain's only SSSI designated specifically for these birds. Although local authorities are legally obliged to protect SSSIs for the benefit of all of us, the developer received the backing of the local Conservative council; after an outcry, the matter was put in the hands of a public inquiry. Britain's nature lovers – a very large constituency, if RSPB membership is taken as a starting point – await its decision.*

So often, nature is portrayed to us as either an obstacle or a luxury, when in fact it's essential to our future wealth

---

* Given the clear strength of public feeling, the planning application was withdrawn ahead of the public inquiry. Medway Council still plans to build five hundred homes outside – but still close to – the SSSI, with subsequent impacts on nightingales and other species.

and well-being – something all the most exciting and imaginative planning projects recognise. Fighting to keep our land green and pleasant is far from regressive; in fact, is one of the most forward-thinking things any nation can do.

13 June 2015

Even in spring, when birdsong is at its most varied and lovely, I cherish the unmusical tweeting of a local gang of cockney sparrows as they racket around our back garden and squabble over the seed feeder. They used to roost communally in next door's yard, which was full of junk and, consequently, nesting places; since it was tidied up they've moved to the eaves of a tall house two doors down, from where, on sunny mornings, they gossip and fuss and scold the passers-by below. I can only hope the house's owners look kindly on their cheerful but noisy guests.

House sparrows were everywhere when I was a child, so ubiquitous as to be almost invisible; now, the tiny group my London street supports is vitally important to a population that has crashed in recent years – in London and across the country too. Each year I send my records in to the Big Garden Birdwatch and wait for the results to be published, hoping sparrow numbers will start to recover. It hasn't happened yet.*

---

* Sparrow numbers, though still far lower than they once were, appear to be recovering in Scotland, Wales and Northern Ireland (but not England), according to Breeding Bird Survey data.

In the nineteenth century sparrows were everywhere in the capital, living on grain fed to horses and spilled at the breweries and grain barges, and forming vast flocks at London Zoo and in the Royal Parks. But by the millennium they had entirely gone from most of inner London's green spaces, with huge declines in private gardens too; they fell by 58 per cent between 1979 and 2015. The reasons are complex and may include changes in farmland management, particularly for suburban populations; greater predation, notably by cats; increased pollution, including noise pollution; modern buildings that offer birds far fewer nesting sites; and a dearth of invertebrates on which sparrows feed their young.

This last possibility is perhaps the most worrying, because its effect, if proven, could well be hitting not just sparrows but the entire food web. The RSPB's London House Sparrow Parks Project aims to discover whether boosting insect numbers by planting wildflowers and letting grass grow long and set seed can have a knock-on effect on sparrow populations; if so, our predilection for paving over urban front gardens, our reliance on insecticides and weedkillers and our preference for a tidily mown sward in public green spaces may be in large part to blame.

I've long been interested in animal bones and recently managed to add an adult fox skull to my small but growing collection – something of a coup. The first fox carcass I ever found had disappeared by the time I returned with latex gloves and garden tools, while the second skull proved not to be intact – it was that of a juvenile, and probably the cranial plates hadn't fused. It might also have been rolled on by a dog. Possibly mine.

This find, though, proved to be third time lucky: a big dog fox that had already decayed to near-skeletal form, saving me a lot of potentially gruesome work. Tartar on the big carnassial teeth suggested that it had reached a good age, and I was able to replace a missing canine with one from the juvenile skull that had fallen apart – not museum practice, but who's to know?

I don't do this enough to invest in dermestid beetles and a tank, and the one time I tried cold-water maceration the smell was enough to put me off for life – though the result, a handful of rat's bones as tiny and perfect as jewels, did make it worth it. Burying in a large, lidded bin full of earth works well for me, followed by careful cleaning with dilute peroxide.

There are pockets of South London that seem utterly rural: paths edged with cow parsley and dog roses and over-hung by oaks through which the sunlight filters down, green-dappled and shifting. I can walk from one blackcap's song to another's, no buildings or roads in sight, breathing in the smell of spring and green growth. At this time of year everything seethes with life: the nettles are thick with aphids, pollen rides the warm June air, the undergrowth is busy with baby birds and cuckoo spit froths overnight. It feels intoxicating.

Because of the long school holidays, determined by a harvest children are no longer required to help bring in, it can feel as though August is summer's apex – but in terms of wild nature, late May and early June are a truer apogee. The grass is lush and green, whereas August will yellow it to thatch; by then, most of our birdsong, and our wildflowers, will be over too. We can extend the flowering period in our gardens by importing plants from other climates, but we lose something when we forget to stop and enjoy the fleeting high points of our natural year.

11 July 2015

Like most Londoners, I orientate myself by the Thames. Living south of the river carries a freight of earned and unearned meanings and becomes a vector in the localised identity politics the capital half-jokingly indulges in. Travelling across the city, one learns to think about the bridges: funnel points for traffic, as well as the best places to find democratically available views.

What's harder to keep in mind is that the Thames is a living waterway as well as a geographical feature: Europe's least polluted metropolitan estuary, in fact, and winner of the prestigious Thiess International Riverprize in 2010. Since being declared biologically dead in the 1950s and cleaned up in the 1960s it's become a nursery ground for many types of fish, including mullet, Dover sole and sea bass, as well as being a vital migratory corridor. Under that inscrutable, silt-coloured surface lies an unseen world of living things.

At this time of year, as we Londoners stream over and under the river in cabs, buses, Tube trains and on foot, tiny sea bass not much more than a centimetre long are arriving from the North Sea and battling their way as far as Richmond, where they'll remain, feeding and putting on weight, until early autumn. There are even tinier flounders thronging the river right now too, using the intertidal foreshore that appears at low tide as a series of stepping stones and 'surfing' upstream – despite barely being able to swim properly yet. In recent years, conservationists have worked closely with Thames Water and other agencies to ensure that wastewater outflows into the river don't disrupt the ability of these tiny fry to get upstream. Given the huge development pressures on the estuary, our ability to ensure the Thames is a clean and living river is something we should be extremely proud of.

And yet the received wisdom is that it is heavily polluted; despite the cormorants, herons and gulls, the idea of its toxicity is deeply ingrained. When seals are seen at Waterloo Bridge, or harbour porpoises in Lambeth, there's not only surprise but misplaced consternation: surely they'll quickly die? Part of it, perhaps, is our lack of access to the water: with little or no experiential understanding of it, the Thames becomes a blank space on to which we project wider fears about the city itself. I'd like to see greater public access to the foreshore, with schoolchildren going out in glass-bottomed boats and species identification boards where the Thames Clippers dock. I'd like the Thames to come alive again in Londoners' minds.

Where the grass has been allowed to grow long on my local common it is suddenly abuzz with *Orthoptera*. We have twenty-seven native grasshoppers, crickets and springtails in the UK, with more and more species now making a home in London and the south-east as rising global temperatures allow them to breed and slowly extend their range.

Despite how loud they sound, the grasshoppers on the common are difficult to spot. As soon as I look in their direction, it seems, they still their zithers; if I see one clinging to a stem it dematerialises the second I approach. Yet National Biodiversity Network records show that seventeen species have been reported on the common, including several non-natives like Roesel's bush-cricket; disappointingly, I've only seen field and meadow grasshoppers so far.

As a rough guide, crickets differ from grasshoppers in having long antennae and being mainly nocturnal. Last summer, one stridulated loudly on every warm, dry night from the tangled front garden of a house on my street, a reminder of how important even small gardens can be. Probably a dark bush-cricket – though I didn't think it wise to investigate – its song lent my evening dog walks a beguilingly subtropical air.

On Wednesday at about five o'clock I heard a blackbird in full song in Covent Garden. It was a warm afternoon, and Neal Street was thronged with shoppers and tourists; from Long Acre and Seven Dials came the sound of taxis and the ding of pedicabs' importunate bells. And poured over it all was that lovely liquid warble, full-throated and rich: a male blackbird declaring that the area was his territory, and his alone. It stopped me in my tracks.

I wonder where his nest is: one of the shrubs in Odham's Walk, or a tree that flanks the 'actor's church', St Paul's? I wonder if he and his mate have successfully reared chicks this year: West End birds, canny and street-smart. Perhaps they are on to their second, or even third, brood. I hope so: streets without birds are a wretched and lifeless thing.

Much of the moment's significance came from knowing that soon all our blackbirds will fall silent until next spring. The brevity of the period in which they sing seems to intensify their song's beauty, a reminder that despite all the conveniences of city living some seasonal events must be enjoyed in the moment, or not at all.

8 August 2015

I'm in Dorset for two weeks, looking after a friend's house with a large garden, orchard and section of riverbank. I come every August, *sans* husband and Scout, leaving

London behind for a glimpse of a very different life.

There are water voles on the river nearby, and last year I had the pleasure of watching one for several minutes while walking the family's Labrador a mile or so from the house. Partly because of this, my friends have recently begun to 'rewild' their stretch of bank so that now, in contrast to some of the manicured but environmentally sterile riverside lawns in evidence nearby, the vegetation in the lower part of their garden has been left to grow, and as two bankside willows reach the end of their natural life several saplings, grown from cuttings, are getting ready to take their place. Since I was last here, water voles have begun to be seen at the end of the garden.

Having spotted some holes on the opposite bank, I positioned a garden chair among the tall grass, nettles, comfrey and greater willowherb, and returned later that afternoon with binoculars and a glass of wine. I tiptoed cautiously to my viewing point – but not cautiously enough. Two splashes, and two arrowing shapes to the shadows of the far bank: a pair of voles had dropped from an overhanging willow branch, where they were feeding, and swum away. I'll go down every day while I'm here in hopes of seeing them again.

These round-faced, chestnut-brown creatures are so charismatic that it's no surprise they inspire such enthusiasm in so many. Yet for all this good feeling, water voles are Britain's fastest-declining mammal. Loss of habitat is a large part of the problem, as ditches and channels are clumsily dredged and stream-side vegetation cut back by landowners and local councils; predation by mink is another factor. A clear national picture is needed to help find ways to reverse their loss; volunteer surveyors are asked to register with the People's Trust for Endangered Species at www.ptes.org.

As well as the busy voles, the garden here dances with butterflies, while dragonflies and azure damselflies flicker over the water and grass snakes bask among the vegetables. Making sure their little corner of Dorset is a home for wildlife, as well as people, is an act of true stewardship, and I admire it immensely.

There's a smart new beehive in the orchard here, though as yet no swarm has been persuaded to move in. But from the kitchen window I can see common carders and solitary bees working the flower borders with their swaying verbena, fat *Echinops* and blowsy roses, and bumblebees visiting the thyme by the house.

There are over two hundred and fifty species of wild bee in Britain, and they are vital to the 80 per cent of wildflowers and crops that rely on insects for pollination. Worryingly, new evidence from Sweden shows that wild bees are even more sensitive to neonicotinoids, used in agriculture, than honeybees, so it's vital we understand what role these pesticides play in their current decline. Yet, as the oilseed rape harvest comes in it looks like being a bumper year – despite this year's seeds not having been treated with these chemicals. Buglife CEO Matt Shardlow has said in a statement, 'This is further evidence that neonicotinoids are not essential to maintaining crop yields.'

It wasn't long ago that the pesticide DDT was being hailed as essential for farming, while all the time it was decimating wild birds. Had we not banned it – following sustained campaigning from conservation groups – we truly would have had a silent spring; I hope we do not one day usher in a beeless summer.

Many birds are now in moult, and all we'll see of them is a shabby shape scuttling into the undergrowth. This makes August a good time to look for feathers. My collection includes a turquoise tail feather from a parakeet, a blue-grey heron plume and a polka-dotted primary from a great spotted woodpecker. The biggest, and perhaps the best, is from a red kite, and was posted to me by my god-daughter Isabel.

It makes me sad when I hear parents tell children not to touch feathers because they're 'dirty'. Collecting and identifying them is a great way to learn about birds, while to grow up with a sense that nature is a threat rather than a source of pleasure and fascination is a great loss. Feathers are no more dirty than anything else outdoors, and harbour nothing that a bar of ordinary soap can't sort out.

21 September 2015

'Invasion of giant moths hits Britain!' frothed some of the more excitable sections of the press this week. The facts were far less dramatic: the nights of 10–12 September were designated 'Moth Nights' by Butterfly Conservation and the journal *Atropos*, with both lepidopterists and the general public invited to lure moths to their gardens for identification, and submit their results. The much hoped-for palm-sized species mentioned by the tabloids was the convolvulus hawkmoth, a pleasingly photogenic species that arrives in the south of Britain from Europe each autumn, and which did a great job of grabbing media attention for this year's event. The theme, appositely enough, was 'migration'.

Being a fan of both citizen science and moths (they're so much more hipster than butterflies), I set up a slightly Heath Robinson-style trap in my city back garden involving two LED torches, a flowerpot, cling film and an old flannel painted with a sticky 'sugaring' mixture cooked up in accordance with instructions from the Moth Night website. Then, as night fell, I readied my camera, notebook and identification guide to record my results. As a first-timer with admittedly suboptimal equipment, I wasn't expecting a convolvulus hawkmoth, of course, but I was hoping for something interesting: an angle shades, perhaps, a satellite or a red-green carpet (which feeds on deciduous trees, not floor coverings).

I got nothing. No moths on the first night, or the second, or the third. Frustratingly, a couple did flutter around my lit living room window, as they do on most evenings, but didn't settle long enough for me to identify them – and none at all visited my sugaring station.

Records are still coming in, and this year's full results will eventually appear in *Atropos*. But word has it other London recorders did far better than me, with at least one report of the migratory vestal moth coming in from Wimbledon, where the old lady, or black underwing, was also seen. If you're curious, the #mothnight hashtag on Twitter is a good way to get a glimpse of the action.

As well as the wine or ale used to make the sugaring mixture, the convolvulus hawkmoth shows a distinct predilection for nicotiana (tobacco) plants, seeds of which had been sent out by the *Atropos* journal to its readers earlier in the year. Surely even lepidopterophobics must warm to a moth with a taste for fags and booze.

Blackberry season is drawing to a close in the capital, though my friends in the north tell me theirs are still going strong. Last weekend I found a hidden cache of them deep in a bramble thicket near Chesham in Buckinghamshire, far out at the very furthest reaches of the Metropolitan line; they were the only ones left there that hadn't gone over. Like dark, clustered garnets holding all summer's sweetness, I find them impossible to pass by.

Each September my husband and I pick as many as we

can from our local parks and fill our freezer so we can make blackberry-and-apple crumble all winter, and we sometimes scrump pears from a tree around the corner that drops sad, smashed fruit on the pavement every year.

Although I see one or two other blackberry pickers out with their Tupperwares, urban foragers are thin on the ground. It seems a shame: more than just a source of free food, foraging for fruit connects us to the natural world and to the seasons, and that's something we city-dwellers often lack.

A great spotted woodpecker has begun to visit our bird feeder. Although they have a reputation for being bold and fearless, ours seems only to slip in very briefly when the house sparrow gang isn't around. With their smart black-and-white uniform and crimson bums they're utterly distinctive, even when glimpsed bouncing away into the sycamore at the end of the garden.

Amid a general picture of steep and widespread species loss within our lifetimes, it's heartening to think that one or two birds are bucking the trend, and the GSW, as it's known in birding circles, is one of them. The UK population increased by 268 per cent between 1970 and 2010 and this upturn has been reflected in the capital. It's now thought that London has several hundred pairs, including a few in the centre of town – one outside the offices of my publisher, in Bedford Square. One factor in their success is believed to be the increase in garden bird feeders, particularly those featuring peanuts: proof that the small changes we make for nature really do make a difference.

10 October 2015

Having a dog can really transform how you think about the place where you live. In my pre-Scout days, the London I lived in seemed dominated by steel and glass, but now I feel I live in a very green city, because I am out walking her so often: either doing the rounds of our local parks, with all the opportunities that brings to see the seasons slowly change, or discovering new places that broaden my picture of what the capital is really like.

Last weekend we drove to Farthing Downs, a rolling chalk escarpment in Coulsdon with breathtaking views. Along with nearby sites New Hill, Devilsden Wood, Eight Acres Common and the aptly named Happy Valley, it's a real rural idyll, and on a fine autumn day it's almost impossible to believe that you're in Greater London at all.

As we walked I listened out for skylarks singing over its central ridge, while Scout raced madly around flushing rabbits from the thickets and grinning. There are crepuscular yew woods, badger setts, woodcock and the slotted prints of shy roe deer, while an Iron Age enclosure and Anglo-Saxon barrows testify to our long relationship with this place.

Every April the woods there glow with bluebells, while in May hawthorn blossom dresses the deep hedgerows, pulling the branches down with its weight. We last went in June, when the meadows glowed golden with greater yellow-rattle, loved by bumblebees; in fact, much of the UK's remaining wild population of this annual meadow plant grows at this site. Because greater yellow-rattle is semi-parasitic and can weaken grass, it was once thought of by farmers as a pest; now, though, we value it for its delicate beauty, and for the job it does in preventing grass from dominating the few fragments of flowering meadow we have left.

Happy Valley and Farthing Downs are a Site of Special Scientific Interest and are progressively and sensitively managed for wildlife and for people by a partnership of organisations including the Downlands Trust and the City of London Corporation. Successional scrub is treated as a habitat in its own right, rather than being eradicated, cattle and sheep are brought in to graze, and the grass is mown late in the year to allow wildflowers to set seed. That's why, despite it being autumn now, the grasslands there are striped with long, unseasonal windrows of hay, while the hedgerows are studded with blue autumn sloes and the woods show the first signs of turning yellow and gold. It's a magical landscape, a real *locus amoenus*, and to me it is just as much a part of London as the Shard.

Another inhabitant of this unusual place is the Roman snail, and in the damper and shadier parts of the woods around Farthing Downs I sometimes find their large, ridged, empty shells, tawny when young but turning paler with age. *Helix pomatia* means 'pot lid snail', though one of its common names, the apple snail, is mistakenly derived from *pomatia*. Lovers of chalky, lime-rich soil, Roman snails go into hibernation at about this time each year, burrowing down into the soil and using calcium derived from the local geology to make a hard but porous lid called an epiphragm to seal themselves up inside their shells. This clever adaptation, which also allows them to aestivate in very dry weather, can help them survive for as long as eight years. They are hermaphrodites whose beautiful and complex mating dance can last up to twenty-four hours, and sometimes results in both partners shooting a calcium 'love dart' into one another's flesh. On the International Union for the Conservation of Nature's Red List of Threatened Species, Roman snails are protected, making it illegal to kill, harm or take them from the wild.

At this time of year wild clematis earns one of its common names: old-man's-beard. Once its flowering period is over, the sweet-smelling white blooms become silky balls of fluff that aid dispersal of its windblown seeds. A vigorous climber, it can ascend trees up to about forty feet, creating cataracts of soft silvery seeds. In Happy Valley its tufts were turning swathes of the hedgerows smoke-grey.

The poet and essayist Edward Thomas loved wild clematis, not least for its other name, the one he preferred:

traveller's joy. He was an inveterate walker, in love with chalk country and drawn to the dream of a life on the road, and it crops up again and again in his work. It wreathed the hedges encircling the house in which he grew up, and in 1913 he planted it at the little cottage he moved to at Steep in Hampshire, where he began to write poetry shortly before enlisting.

When tinder-dry, the seed heads of traveller's joy make excellent kindling; country wisdom holds that they can also be used to create a soft pillow should one ever find oneself spending a night on the road.

14 November 2015

I got the train to Essex to see a badger named Barry, but Barry failed to materialise; and sometimes, with wildlife, that's how it goes.

Bazza the Badger, as I decided to call him (another soubriquet was coined following his no-show), visits my friend David's back garden nightly – except when David has invited anyone to see him. Sometimes Barry brings the wife too. They haul themselves under the fence and snuffle up peanuts David leaves on his patio, tripping the security light so everyone in the house knows to look out of the patio doors. But while I'm there the garden remains dark, the peanuts untouched.

Barry has a sett not far away, in a chalk bank where, in summer, sand martins nest; a clear trail created by the regular passage of a low-slung animal leads from the bank through the grass to the back of the gardens. The area was a chalk quarry before houses were built there around the turn of the millennium; not far away is a place called Badgers Dene, suggesting that these charismatic creatures have lived in the area for a very long time.

Books and TV programmes about wildlife often imply a far greater hit rate than most of us actually experience, because they tend to concentrate on the moment of encounter rather than the hours of waiting around, or the failed trips, like mine. Similarly, they're unequivocal about identification, leaving out the part where the writer or filmmaker consulted several field guides, or listened to a bird's unusual-sounding alarm call eighteen times on an app, or phoned a friend. (This does happen, even among experts.) But this erasure of failure and doubt distorts the picture, making it seem as though animals appear on demand for the experts and are a cinch to ID. Instead of learning patience and fieldcraft, it's tempting for the rest of us to conclude that we just don't have the skills, and leave wildlife-spotting to those who do. And that's a shame.

And there's another problem with how easy it is to encounter nature second-hand, via books and TV: it implies an abundance that no longer reflects reality. *Springwatch* and *Autumnwatch* presenter Martin Hughes-Games has admitted as much, saying that wildlife programmes have created 'a form of entertainment, a utopian world that bears no resemblance to the reality'. We need to understand that the reason it can be hard to see, for example, glow-worms or yellowhammers, is not necessarily that we lack expertise; it's that we have, in this country, and within a generation, all but wiped them out.

It's been a good year for autumn colour, but now wind is stripping the leaves from the trees. On London's streets they skitter around in eddies and pile up in drifts; after rain, Scout stops often to bury her nose in the damp piles where smells linger. Here and there the paving slabs are stained with ghost leaves: tea-coloured shapes where anthocyanins and carotenoids have bled out, leaving marks that persist for weeks. On the common, the mud under the tannin-rich oaks is blacker than the surrounding earth; where puddles form, they have an iridescent film from the plant oils being released.

My little garden is choked with the leaf-fall from two sycamores, my damson tree and two *Prunus nigra*. As fast as we bag them up, more appear, clotting the fences and borders like a tide. They make the garden look unkempt, but I remind myself that dead leaves are new soil in the making: saprotrophic fungi, slime moulds, bacteria and invertebrates will soon release the nutrients they contain, and in the meantime they are much picked-over by birds.

We take decomposition for granted, but possibly the most chilling news to come out of the forests near

Chernobyl is the fact that dead trees and leaf litter are barely decaying, because radiation has wiped out the detritivores in the soil. Each year, more leaves fall – and there they remain: a near-inert carpet now twenty-nine autumns deep.

Twice a year billions of the world's birds obey the call to migrate, undertaking unimaginably perilous journeys in order to breed, survive the winter or seek food. Broadly following eight intercontinental flyways, birds of all species and sizes share the skies as they navigate the globe. These vast biannual shifts are one of the great wonders of the natural world, and one of them is happening right now, in the skies over our heads. Walking Scout late at night I hear Scandinavian redwings calling to one another above the city streets; their remains, along with those of snipe and other migrants, are turning up at urban peregrine roosts. Twitter updates from the London Bird Club and the British Trust for Ornithology show an influx of short-eared owls from Russia and Iceland, as well as firecrests from Fennoscandia.

At just six grams it's amazing firecrests can survive such a journey – though of course many die en route. Freezing temperatures kill them even more certainly, though, so for those facing winter in colder countries than Britain, the risks of a two-thousand-kilometre journey must be worth it.

19 December 2015

This week a friend came across a grey partridge that had been killed by a car in the road near her Suffolk home. In a photo it lies unmarked upon her table, beak very slightly open, bright eyes closed. The greys and browns of its plumage are a miracle of precision: the colour of twigs and winter earth, the cross-hatching of dead wood at the bottom of a hedge.

Only a little death, you might think, but it matters: these plump, shy ground birds, native to these isles and mostly known to us now from the 'Twelve Days of Christmas' carol, are a UK Red List species, and we haven't many left. This bird was one of a covey living in fallow fields near my friend's home, but in recent weeks developers have torn the fields up and made the partridges homeless. Without a field to forage in, this covey could well now be lost.

The reasons for grey partridges' decline are complex, but two factors in particular stand out. After the Second World War a demand for greater food production led to thousands of miles of hedgerows being grubbed up and the field margins cultivated; new strains of cereals allowed for winter sowing too. Our agricultural land lost the ancient hedges, wildflower meadows and unregarded corners where partridges used to live. At the same time, farmers began to use new chemicals to eradicate crop weeds. Many of those weeds supported the invertebrates that chicks feed on in their early weeks of life, and without them broods began to fail – not just those of partridges, but of other farmland birds too. In making the countryside work so hard for humans, its ability to support other creatures began to be lost.

The UK's steep decline in invertebrate numbers is perhaps the most terrifying part of this story: in the last thirty-five years, as biocide use has soared, we have lost nearly half their number. It isn't so much a question of extinctions – though there have been plenty – but of abundance. There is simply less of everything: fewer butterflies, currently at a forty-year low; fewer moths and bees and hoverflies and beetles than when you and I were young. The ramifications of this could well prove catastrophic, not just for birds but for all life on earth; we have to find a way to put it right.

When the parson-naturalist Gilbert White began recording the wildlife in his Hampshire parish of Selborne in 1768, he couldn't have known that his notes would lead to the science of ecology: the study of interactions between organisms and their environment. White was not the only gentleman amateur to further our knowledge of the natural world, but he differed from his contemporaries in that he observed animals in their own habitats, allowing him to grasp their complex interdependence on other living things.

In recent years we've begun to understand that we are ourselves habitats, our bodies home to vast and varied populations of organisms that together form our microbiome. They have evolved in partnership with us for millennia, and make up 1–3 per cent of our body weight; they are (strange to think) as much a part of the natural world as robins and red deer. And far from being harmful or even unnecessary to us, it's now thought that a healthy, balanced microbiome is vital for everything from good digestion to allergy prevention, a well-functioning auto-immune response and even our mental health.

We may prefer not to think about these tiny organisms, but we need them nonetheless – just as our countryside needs bees and disappearing butterflies, and the grey partridges, common in Gilbert White's day, that are now so rarely seen.

In London, during a mild December, winter can be hard to see and feel. The grass of the parks and verges remains green, the easy-care *Photinia*, laurels and privets in the housing estates, car parks and roundabouts keep their leaves, and in air-conditioned office blocks the temperature holds steady until spring. Where you can see it is in the trees, though, whose bare black branches spend the short days etched against a dull midwinter sky.

Mature London planes are decorated for the season with seed balls like dangling baubles; leafless ash trees are distinguishable by their recurved twigs that bow and beckon up. The silhouettes of sycamores and oaks can look similar from a distance, until you draw close enough

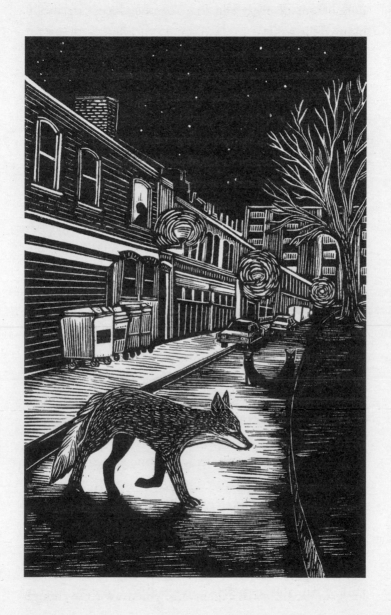

to see the bark: scaly and flaky for sycamores, vertically fissured for oaks.

In the naked trees, birds can be more easily seen: coal-black crows hunched and cawing, fat wood pigeons grey as clouds, dapper magpies angling the levers of their tails between twigs. Living and lovely, they dress the city's winter branches like the bird-shaped ornaments that hang on my Christmas tree at home.

23 January 2016

When I was very small, my father, who commuted into central London every day from our Surrey home, would count the rabbits he saw from the train on his way back in the evening – or at least, would reply to my questions with a likely-sounding number. Sometimes he'd tell me about the herons, deer and foxes he'd seen too, so accustomed to the railway line as to ignore the metal tube full of exhausted office workers hurtling by. I still love spotting wildlife from trains, and always keep my eyes open – although on my way to Wales last year a lone ostrich, belting away from the tracks across open pasture, came as something of a surprise.

In autumn and winter Dad would often tell me about the starlings too: huge murmurations that would fold and billow over the city skyline, and the long flight lines he'd see heading to their roosts in Trafalgar Square and Regent's Park. Adaptable and clever, they seemed to cope well in cities, despite concerted attempts to disrupt their roosts. (In 1949 a large flock settled on the Houses of Parliament, stopping the hands of Big Ben's clock for four and a half minutes.) Flocks could be huge; in December 1968, one in Bromley was estimated by a recorder for the London Natural History Society to consist of close to a million birds; it 'stretched from one horizon to the other and came over as a continuous band for an appreciable time'.

Since then starling numbers have collapsed by 80 per cent nationwide; it's thought that juveniles struggle to find enough invertebrates to eat, and simply starve to death. This could be behind the recent decline in house sparrows too. The reason for the lack of invertebrates? Among other things, our reliance on insecticides and weedkillers, the fashion for paving and decking our gardens, and the steep decline in unmown, unweeded bits of land full of the plants that bugs need to live. Largely unnoticed, invertebrates' current crash is affecting everything further up the chain.

To see starlings in big numbers I'd have to take a train far out of the city now. Yet there are a few about, their population boosted right now by visiting birds from Scandinavia. I see them in our local park, teams of a dozen or so probing the muddy grass like little pitch inspectors. They are dull from a distance, audible by clicks and ribald whistles, but up close as glossy and iridescent as clockwork toys.

Researchers at the University of York and the John Innes Centre report that they have identified the genetic markers that predict a low level of susceptibility to the deadly ash dieback disease, or *Chalara fraxinea*. While the progress of the disease cannot be halted, nor infected trees saved, this increases the possibility that we could replant resistant saplings as the UK's current population dies. Every time I see an ash on my nearby common – some whippy youngsters, some graceful, mature specimens hung with bunches of seeds – I wonder how long they have left.

Ash trees are relied on by over nine hundred other species, from bullfinches to bats. That's because, unlike more recent introductions, they have lived here for millennia, and in that time have evolved alongside everything else. Sometimes the call to protect Britain's native species from invaders can be framed a little jingoistically, but the truth is we need the things that belong here in order to make our ecosystem work.

At last, this week we had some proper winter weather. Average temperatures in December were closer to those of April or May, and for a while it seemed as though a mild, wet autumn was simply going to give way to spring. It felt unnerving.

Cold weather prompts creatures to hibernate that otherwise won't find much to eat, and kills off pests and pathogens – including, I hope, the unseasonal mosquito that bit me several times last week. Many plants need to stop growing for a time too; a warm winter can weaken them for the next growing year.

Yet some have been fooled: there are ornamental cherries in bloom across the city, and here and there daffodils are out. Once, wild daffodils carpeted meadows close to London, much as bluebells do in woods today; in the 1930s, Daffodil Specials took Londoners by train to the Herefordshire–Gloucestershire border to walk among the 'golden tide'.

Modern cooling techniques now take the place of winter frosts and help ensure commercially grown daffs are in the supermarkets when we want them. In a jug on my desk they are no less cheerful for it; yet how much more magical is the wild kind, clinging on in scattered colonies across the British Isles.

27 February 2016

On a bright, chilly February lunchtime with blue skies, a stiff breeze and the first skylark of the year singing somewhere overhead, I picked up the bulbous spine of *Pseudocidaris mammosa*, a sea urchin that lived and died when dinosaurs walked (and swam, and flew over) the earth – and which had waited for me to find it, in Peterborough, ever since.

I had taken the East Coast Main Line out of King's Cross to meet the zoologist Jules Howard, author of *Death on Earth: Adventures in Evolution and Mortality*. Peterborough seemed an unlikely place to find fossils – one always thinks of the coast – but he had assured me that there was a site just outside the city centre where we'd easily find some. 'Shall I bring a trowel?' I'd asked by email. 'No need!' he'd replied. Sitting on the train, the East Midlands whizzing past, the whole enterprise had seemed mystifying and unlikely.

And yet it was true. As soon as I had got my eye in, it seemed that the pointed tubes of belemnites – my childhood obsession due to their old country name of elf arrows – lay everywhere amid the flints, thorny scrub and burst cartridge cases of the strange and stripped-back landscape Jules had introduced me to. Crouching to focus in close, I found a few radially symmetrical stalk fragments of crinoids: strange marine animals that are sometimes known as sea lilies. Jules, meanwhile, was picking up gnarled *Gryphaea* ('devil's toenails'), tube-worm exoskeletons and what we both hoped might prove to be a small shark coprolite, or poo. 'You need to imagine all this,' he said, gesturing around us and grinning, 'as a Jurassic seabed.'

Built on rich Oxford clay, Peterborough was once famous for its brickworks and there are many abandoned clay quarries and pits around the city, some filled in and built over, some converted to leisure use and some now precious wildlife reserves. Where the sedimentary clay remains exposed – as at our site, just off the Green Wheel cycleway – the marine fossils it held on to for so long lie at the surface like messages from another time, another earth.

We talked about death, not morbidly but curiously – it was hard not to, walking as we were among the remains of millions of individuals whose existences had played out no less intricately or dramatically than our own. Human life felt small and fleeting, and it wasn't frightening but a comfort: a reminder that whatever our depredations, the Anthropocene, like the Jurassic, will pass.

The ponds scattered across this post-industrial site were home to stoneworts, uniquely complex aquatic algae that looked to my untrained eye like a nondescript sort of pondweed. Seven species are found in Peterborough's old brick pits, including the vanishingly rare bearded stonewort, which only exists in a few locations in the entire UK.

Here's what's truly extraordinary, though: these primitive organisms are 400 million years old, and are perhaps the missing evolutionary link between algae and non-vascular plants, which then developed, over millennia, into violets and oak trees, orchids and rye grass and everything green that grows on land. And they weren't planted: they just colonised the ponds and flooded brick pits, ancient pioneer species that may one day disappear again if the water, low in nutrients, becomes too rich. The stoneworts swaying in the chill margins of the pond were delicate, living fossils – just as fascinating as the long-dead cephalopods and sea urchins we'd been hunting for in the clay.

It was hard to leave; I was haunted by the possibility that a more complete ammonite – or perhaps a shark's tooth, or a plesiosaur bone! – lay waiting if we only searched a little longer. And then, across the water, rose another creature from a different time: a red kite, one of the UK's great conservation success stories, lit orange by the low winter sun.

Famously – as Shakespeare could have told you – red kites live mostly by scavenging, eating the carcasses of creatures that would otherwise rot and spoil, or perhaps pass down to become part of a new fossil record for future, unimaginable life forms to find. Strange to think that the red kite, Jules and I were all at the brick pits for the same reason; all of us scanning the bleak clay for lost lives.

2 April 2016

It's been a sewage farm, a training ground for the local civil defence unit, and a pottery and brickworks; vast amounts of rubble was dumped there following the Blitz. But on Bank Holiday Monday, I stood in South Norwood Country Park in South London and heard a Cetti's warbler sing.

This low-lying, wet, forty-seven-hectare site opened as a Local Nature Reserve in 1989 and now boasts bat and butterfly walks and dawn chorus outings, while volunteers meet for monthly work days to clear scrub and brambles, plant trees and carry out conservation work. For both people and wildlife it is a precious urban resource.

We may have been in SE25 but Scout was in countryside mode: she put up a brace of pheasants, stalked small mammals in the undergrowth and streaked off after a big dog fox. All the while a kestrel hovered over us, working hard to keep still in the last of Storm Katie's winds. But it was the Cetti's warbler that made my day: my third ever, and the first I've identified on my own. Belting out from dense briars edging the water, its strident and unmistakable song stopped me in my tracks. Excitedly checking the BirdTrack website, I could see I was the second person in recent days to report one there.

This little bird has come to us from the Continent, first breeding here in 1973; there are still only thought to be two thousand pairs, mostly near the coasts of the south-east, south-west and East Anglia, but slowly making inroads into the rest of the British Isles. The mild winter we've had in the south will have been good for them; they don't cope well in the cold.

Cetti's warblers are shy and hard to see, and without hearing this one I'd never have known it was there. But a year ago I would have walked past without recognising its song, and five years before that I'd never even heard of them – I'd probably just have thought it was a wren. For me, learning to recognise birds and their songs is about making the world richer: spring, now, isn't just about generalised birdsong, but particular birds in particular spots. Each year I learn to recognise a couple more; each year my local streets and parks become more interesting places. It's like a magic trick.

They come around with depressing regularity: scare stories about animals that are freakishly large, or deadly, or supposedly rampaging around. Last month it was the turn of a 'mutant' rat in Hackney, handily disposed of before the story could be disproved. No matter: it was confidently proclaimed to be four feet long and twenty-five pounds, and much was made of its proximity to 'an area where children play'. Some believe it was a foreign species, brought here as bushmeat or for a pet; the photo has been shown to employ clever use of perspective to increase its size. One thing is certain: it was not a four-foot-long brown rat. Small wonder, though, that city kids can be wary of wildlife, when this is what they're told.

Why do we get such a kick out of reading and sharing this nonsense? Do we miss, at some level, having proper predators to fear; or do these beliefs justify in our minds our desire to harm some animals, or allay the guilt that human destructiveness provokes?

This week, blue tits have been investigating one of my garden boxes, while on Twitter photos are circulating of the year's first long-tailed tit nests: stretchy, teardrop-shaped constructions made of lichen, moss and spider silk. Meanwhile, building work has just finished on my local church, and I'll be watching to see whether the swifts that raise chicks there every year are still able to find somewhere to nest.

Many birds that have spent centuries learning to live alongside us, like house sparrows, swallows, house martins and swifts, are struggling now that modern building techniques and materials no longer allow them access; at the same time, many countryside roosting and breeding sites are being lost. One answer is bird boxes integrated into buildings, such as those provided by innovative Sussex company Bird Brick Houses: neat, brick-matched and predator-proof, with an impressive 75 per cent take-up rate. It would be a real step forward if developers were required by local councils to provide homes for displaced birds and bats.

7 May 2016

East London isn't where you'd expect to see Sir David Attenborough gazing out across eleven hectares of wetland where great crested grebes dance on the water, little egrets hunt the shallow margins and reed buntings and warblers sing from dense reed beds, but that was the scene last weekend when Woodberry Wetlands was at last opened to the public, with over two thousand people streaming in. It may be surrounded by high-rise buildings rather than picture-book countryside, but with frogs, bats, rare damselflies and nearly fifty bird species being recorded per day during the last fortnight, it's more than proved its worth as a home for wildlife – and can now provide much-needed breathing space for people too.

In his speech Sir David hailed Woodberry as a beacon of hope, an example of things in the natural world getting better rather than worse. He lauded the opportunity it creates 'for children to see the seasons as they pass; to see not just asphalt and concrete and brick, but reeds and willows; to see birds coming up here from Africa; to hear, above the hubbub of the traffic, birdsong; to catch a glimpse of a kingfisher, one of the most wonderful sights that Britain has to offer – that flash of blue as it flies upriver'.

A place like Woodberry proves there's no need for any urban child to be denied these wonders, or for anywhere, no matter how built-up, to be a wildlife desert. With a little ambition and imagination we can bring nature right into the heart of our cities. Strange and wonderful, thronged with life, Woodberry Wetlands shows what we can achieve when we try.

Its name derives from Old English *dægeseage* and means 'day's eye', for the way it opens its petals at sunrise and closes them at dusk, and May is a good month in which to reacquaint oneself with the humblest of all our native wildflowers. Daisies star the spring grass of London's parks and verges, their low rosettes of leaves safe from mowers and adapted to survive the passage of feet. Traditional gardeners, who hanker over a perfect sward, often curse both daisies and dandelions (from *dent de lion*, meaning 'lion's tooth', for their toothed leaves), but these days more and more people recognise their value to pollinating insects, and enjoy, too, their innocent and somehow nostalgic beauty. For these are probably the flowers most familiar from childhood, when we all spent more time in closer contact with the grass: pushing a thumbnail through a daisy's stem to make what the poet Alice Oswald calls 'a lovely necklace out of her green bones', blowing a dandelion clock to tell the time or watching the bitter white latex ooze from their hollow stems. 'It makes people wet the bed,' my brother would say, gleefully; and indeed dandelion leaves are a diuretic and a key ingredient in the traditional French dish *pissenlit au lard*. We disregard them, as adults, for their ubiquity, but writers and artists from Chaucer to Shakespeare, Albrecht Dürer to William Morris and John Clare to Laurie Lee have loved the 'lawn weeds' for their simple and unpretentious beauty.

On Thursday I saw my first swifts of 2016, carving across London's skies like black scimitars and trailing summer in their wake. I usually spot them a little later than my friends further east or near the coasts, and the day they finally reach me is a highlight of my year.

Swifts cope a little better with cities than house martins or swallows as they can fly higher to avoid pollution; nevertheless, numbers are falling here and elsewhere. They nest at a church and a block of flats near me, and both buildings have had work done during the last twelve months; I'll be devastated if they can't get access to either site. The sound of their screams when I'm gardening spells out summer, and few things are more joyful than their aerial dogfights, swooping almost to street level at breathtaking speed and chasing one another pell-mell through the stagnant city air.

It amazes me that swifts can eat, sleep and mate on the wing, so that come August the chicks will launch themselves into a world made only of air, racing away from London to sub-Saharan Africa and not touching down again for one, two or even three whole years.

11 June 2016

Last weekend we loaded up the car with outdoor gear, settled Scout in the boot and drove north for six hours to the Lakes, where my husband and I spend a week walking each year with his parents. The hawthorn, almost over in South London, was on the turn in Staffordshire; by the time we reached Cumbria it was in full and glorious bloom. In three hundred-odd miles we had turned spring's clock back by about a week.

Watching England unfold on either side of the motorway, I thought about time and its unpredictable effects. Old stone farms which had once been remote now had six lanes of cars roaring past them; rural villages, with their heartbreaking spires, no longer dreamed deep in their meadows but were busy with golf courses, business parks and executive homes. I had the peculiar sense – familiar and beguiling – of the past coexisting with the present; the England that existed for so long and exists no longer haunting the modern landscape, almost close enough to touch.

It was heartening to see so many raptors from the car: red kites over the M40; a kestrel hovering above the central reservation just south of Birmingham, wings working, head pin-sharp and still; then at last, as hills began to rise around us, buzzards soaring on thermals, broad wings motionless against the sky. There are more raptors of almost all kinds now than fifty years ago, thanks to Rachel Carson's 1962 book *Silent Spring* and the subsequent banning of DDT. The past may seem beguiling, but the present has much to recommend it too.

In Glenridding, on Ullswater, the marks of the recent past were everywhere, from the scoured-out river channel to the flood-hit shops. Yet Helvellyn's bulk was just as imposing as always, the valleys and lower slopes clothed, like Alpine meadows, in buttercups, late bluebells, red campion and speedwell. At our rental cottage, built to house lead miners, we unpacked and ate, then sat outside with a drink as dusk fell, forty minutes later than it had fallen on our London flat. The house martins quietened in the eaves and the ewes and lambs in the in-bye fields went to sleep; the long day ended around us, and spring moved inexorably on.

Legend has it that when the great biologist J. B. S. Haldane was asked by a group of theologians what one could conclude as to the nature of God from a study of his creation, Haldane replied, 'An inordinate fondness for beetles.' One can see why, for they constitute about a quarter of all living things, with around four hundred thousand known species worldwide, and over four thousand in the UK.

In southern England it's stag beetle season as the adults emerge from rotting wood, where they have lived as pupae for several years, to seek a mate. Their numbers have declined dramatically since I was a child, when I used to see these magnificent creatures every summer, our ever-tidier gardens and the consequent loss of dead wood habitat thought to be part of the problem. The People's Trust for Endangered Wildlife is asking for our sightings at www.ptes.org.

Less dramatic, but no less interesting, is the rove beetle (*Staphylinus erythropterus*) I discovered halfway up Helvellyn. Fast-moving, brightly marked and with a long, thin body, it looks every inch the fierce little predator it is.

A couple of days before we left for the Lakes, I visited Bethnal Green Nature Reserve in East London, where a project called Phytology is now open to the public for its third year.

In medieval times the land was occupied by a nursery and market garden; as recently as the early 1800s it was still meadow and pasture. In the 1840s it became the site of a church dedicated to St Jude, patron saint of lost causes, but it was destroyed in the Blitz. Untouched, unloved and growing ever wilder, the plot was fenced off until a residents' association began to care for it in the 1990s. It has hosted Phytology, part physic garden, part art project, since 2014.

Steel railings enclose an urgent press of vegetation. Inside, paths loop around chunks of ecclesiastical rubble and wind through luxuriant foliage loud with fledgling birds. Here and there, movement sensors trigger recordings of pieces composed by Phytology's writers-in-residence; there are art installations and a writing hut, as well as ponds and a fox den. An open area hosts performances and meetings, while at one end a small medicinal field is sown with native plants such as comfrey, borage and feverwort, which visitors can harvest for their own use.

It may only be a tiny site but it's dense with history, meaning and purpose, proof of the value to people and wildlife of even the smallest fragment of urban green space.

16 July 2016

Seventeen miles west of central London's loud and strobe-lit clubs, my Friday night out was proving surprisingly exciting. Looking across Frays Farm Meadows as dusk fell, I said, 'I'd like a barn owl now, please' – and within a few minutes one materialised, drifting low over the tall and tangled grass on silent wings. It was an electrifying moment – yet the evening was about to improve. Less than half an hour later the eleven of us were crouched amid the crepuscular vegetation, peering down and laughing, exhilarated, wonderstruck.

'There's one!' – *'Look, there! Amazing!'* – *'There's another over here, come and see!'* What we'd come in hopes of seeing were only some small, odd-looking invertebrates, but it turns out that few things engender

joy like the sight of glow-worms lighting up the mid-summer night.

'Bright scatter'd, twinkling star of spangled earth', the peasant-poet John Clare called them: and they really are like little stars. The light emitted by the abdomen of the female *Lampyris noctiluca* beetle is green, cool and astonishingly bright; like the constellations they do seem distant, their otherworldly glow very concentrated and illuminating almost nothing of the grass and leaves to which they cling. An animal that can make its own light: what an incongruous and utterly bewitching thing.

Our guided walk included three twenty-something women and a couple of local lads, one seventeen, one twenty-two, who had heard about it on Twitter. Some hadn't realised we had glow-worms in this country; many people believe them to be an American phenomenon (the firefly is a relative), or assume they must be long extinct. Numbers have declined since the days of John Clare, but at chalky sites rich in the snails their larvae eat they can still sometimes be found.

Frays Valley Local Nature Reserve is a precious fragment of urban wildness, a mosaic of protected meadows, ancient woodland, waterways and flooded gravel pits bordered by a golf course and the Grand Union Canal. Volunteers have been clearing scrub and invasive goat's-rue from the old railway embankment that bisects it so the glow-worms there can flourish, and Friday night's count proved their hard work is paying off.

All the more dismaying, then, to learn that this magical place is under threat from plans to lay an access road for HS2 across it. Surely another route can be found?

Back in the heart of town a new project aims to boost the numbers of bugs, birds and bats to be found on some of London's busiest shopping streets. Wild West End brings together several large property owners encompassing nearly all of Regent Street, half of St James's, most of Marylebone, three hundred acres of Mayfair and Belgravia, parts of Carnaby Street, Covent Garden, Chinatown, Soho and Charlotte Street and the area between Oxford Street and Edgware Road, extending north and east. Green roofs and walls are to be installed, as well as wildlife-friendly planting schemes, insect habitats, street trees, beehives, vegetable gardens and flower boxes, the aim being to create 'wildlife corridors' linking up areas of fragmented green space, improve local air quality and promote access to nature for people too.

The project will start by establishing the baseline numbers of birds and bats in the area in order to record any increase – particularly in house sparrows, now largely missing from the heart of London, and rare black redstarts, which have successfully bred on one of the green roofs at London's Olympic Park.

On our local common the dense bramble thickets are in bloom, white and grubby pink, and are much visited by bees and hoverflies. I'm hoping for a good blackberry season later in the year; there's something satisfying about filling up on foraged food – especially if you've scrumped the apples too.

The Biological Records Centre, in its plant atlas, calls *Rubus fruticosus* 'taxonomically intractable' – and with good reason. Its position is complex, partly through historical ambiguity and partly due to the fact that its several hundred microspecies mean that it's now often considered an aggregate rather than a single species of plant.

Just as intractable as its taxonomy are the dense, prickly fortresses it creates, its arched canes often rooting where they touch the ground. You may hear me cursing that impenetrability later in the year when I go blackberrying, but bramble clumps act as safe havens for birds and mammals, as well as ensuring that there'll always be some unreachable berries left over for creatures who, let's be honest, need them rather more than I.

20 *August* 2016

August again and I'm back in Dorset for my annual dog-sitting fortnight. At the end of my friends' garden runs a tributary of the River Stour, slow and deep between overgrown banks. One of the great pleasures of my time here is to sit on the little wooden jetty, under an overhanging beech, and do nothing for an hour but watch the water slip slowly by.

Sometimes, something happens: a fish rises and ripples the surface, perhaps a grayling or brown trout; a kingfisher calls *peep*, then flashes past, glinting; a bright-eyed brown rat investigates the exposed roots of an alder on the other bank. Most of the time, though, there is just the cold, slow-moving river bearing the odd dead leaf or feather, the contented notes of a wood pigeon from somewhere high above, and the light sparkling on the water and dappling the undersides of the leaves. My breathing slows, and perhaps my heart; my attention seems to be distilled and focused by the water, rather than its usual distracted scatter. It isn't meditation, I don't think, because my focus is keenly outward; but I'm sure every angler will recognise the feeling I describe.

This year I've seen more members of the order *Odonata* ('toothed ones') on the river than on any previous visit. There are both azure and large red damselflies, and here and there banded demoiselles dance their courtship dances in patches of sunlight, their bodies glinting rich enamel-blue with black-thumbprint wings. One afternoon, while I was sitting quietly on the jetty, a dragonfly – one of the fast-flying hawkers, though I didn't see it for long enough for a firm ID – piloted its way upstream, its purposefulness and manoeuvrability making it look like a small and very beautiful radio-controlled drone; or, perhaps more poetically, a 'gypsy-coloured engine', as the poet Alice Oswald has it.

Back at home in the Big Smoke, the London Wildlife Trust is asking city-dwellers to submit *Odonata* sightings at www.wildlondon.org.uk/dragonfly-detectives. It doesn't matter if you're not sure of the species – all information is welcome. Dragonflies and damselflies are early responders to climate change, and also excellent indicators of clean water, so sightings will help the trust build up a detailed picture of the health of the capital's streams and rivers, lakes and ponds.

In my charge here are four handsome hens, two grey and two white, who arrived a few days before I did to replace the last contingent, who were killed by a fox. They have the run of the garden, going back in the coop around nine at night, whereupon I drag myself away from the book I'm trying to write and go out to lock them in. But at lunchtime on my third day here I heard clucking and looked out of the kitchen window to see a large dog fox raising havoc on the lawn. I let the dogs out, but they charged off in entirely the wrong direction; meanwhile Reynard, unsuccessful this time at least, slipped away.

I see foxes almost every evening in South London: slight, drab shadows slipping between parked cars or trotting silently along street-lit pavements. But whenever I see one in the countryside – which is far less often – I'm struck by their colour: a bright, rich russet, far redder than the ones I see in town. Perhaps the city street lights leach the colour from their coats, or mange – more prevalent in urban populations – makes more of their grey underfur show through. Either way, my wily Dorset visitor was a much more handsome and impressive beast.

*

Settled summer weather has finally given way for most of us to wind and rain, and according to the Met Office autumn will begin on 1 September – though astronomical autumn won't be with us until the equinox, still a month away.

In the garden here the exotic incomers, like globe thistles, crocosmia, tiger lilies and agapanthus, have brought some late-summer colour to the beds, but on my daily dog walks it's been clear our native plants and wildlife know the year is on the turn. Most wildflowers are over, the nettles are limp and spent and the thistles crowned with gouts of pewter down; there is little or no birdsong to be heard, and sloes and hawthorn berries are colouring in the hedges.

In the little orchard down by the river, the Discovery apples blush ruby-red. A Suffolk cultivar, it was bred to ripen early; the others here – including West Country varieties Melcombe Russet, Slack-ma-Girdle and Bridgwater Pippin – are still some way behind. Perhaps autumn will come in by degrees, as the apples do, rather than arriving overnight. Perhaps summer will prove to have some life left in it yet.

24 September 2016

One of the pleasures of a holiday in rural France is the way the landscape and wildlife can feel similar enough to our own as to be decipherable, and yet remain unfamiliar.

The result is a subtly *unheimlich* feeling; no sooner do you pause to admire the bucolic, rolling pastures and woods than you realise no hedgerows cross the hill's flank; and just as you recognise the familiar *dink-dink-dink* of a chiffchaff, a jet-black bee the size of a Nespresso pod hoves into view.

The violet carpenter bee is one of the largest in Europe, with a plumply upholstered, high-shine abdomen and wings like dark smoked glass. Piloting cumbrously around the Gallic countryside, their uniform blackness and loudly whirring wings suggest an apian battle-bot built by Orcs, or perhaps a miniature, flying version of The Beast, President Obama's armoured SUV. In fact they are a gentle species whose name derives from the violet iridescence of their wings when seen in sunlight, and the females' habit of creating tunnels in dead wood in which to lay eggs.

These piano-black pollinators are so much bigger than even the chunkiest of our British bumblebees that the first time you see one it's enough to stop you in your tracks. As our climate warms they may become a more familiar sight, though: since 2007 there's been a small breeding colony in Leicester, with further reports elsewhere.

I was keen to see a hoopoe while in France, having spotted one on a previous trip, but sadly this handsome bird, with its exotic crest of feathers, did not play ball this time. Glorying not only in their British name – a favourite with small children – but also in the agreeable Latin moniker of

Upupa epops, they have the further nomenclatural distinction of harbouring *Upupicola upupae*, a louse.

'Old vaudevillian', Isobel Dixon calls the hoopoe in her poem 'Upupa Epops'; a 'dandy priest' whose rare visits to our southern counties cause 'a flutter on the wires'. True to form, when I returned from France it was to reports on Twitter that one had been found in Bridgwater. The Somerset hoopoe is now being cared for by Secret World Wildlife Rescue, ready for release back into the wild – and hopefully a trip south, to sunnier climes.

We stayed in the Dordogne area, formerly the Périgord, known for its confit de canard, black truffles, chateaux, Bergerac wine, British tourists and Palaeolithic cave art. It's also famous for walnuts, used in everything from salads to desserts and stuffings, aperitifs, digestifs and liqueurs. Demolishing a *tarte aux noix* on our last night, I reminded myself that they can apparently reduce cholesterol – useful, given the cheese I'd been scoffing all week.

Everywhere we passed orchards of these distinctive trees with their broad crowns and dangling green fruits, the views between their trunks going on for a long way. Small wonder: walnuts secrete a chemical called juglone which seeps from their roots and prevents many competing plants from establishing themselves under their canopies. Juglone is also a mild organic pesticide and can evaporate from their leaves on hot days to keep their shade free of insects – something country people everywhere, including in Britain, have long taken advantage of. Although they haven't historically fruited well in our climate, once, walnut trees were planted by farmhouses to tether horses under, so they could be less bothered by flies. Some of these farmyard specimens, though long gone, still haunt the archaeological record as a large black patch of soil, stained by decades of tannins from decaying hulls and leaves.

One of the most satisfying things about knowing a place well is observing how it changes over time. On my local London common I've watched the course of paths alter to avoid wet ground or brambles, the old route slowly grassing over until a newcomer would never know it had been there; tree stumps have decayed over years, colonised by fungi and plants and eventually claimed by the earth until only a hillock remains. One tree fell but lived on, sending up a succession of new vertical branches that is now a row of young trees.

While I was away, parts of the games pitch erupted with yellow flowers to a degree I don't remember seeing before. From a distance they look like a sea of buttercups, and up close like small dandelions; they are in fact autumn hawkbit, a common grassland wildflower. But why the sudden proliferation? Last winter and spring were very wet and parts of the common became waterlogged, the 'stoachy' ground churned up by feet. It's my bet that the hawkbit, a perennial that spreads by seeds, took swift advantage of the gaps the disturbance left in the grass cover, leading months later to this sudden flush of autumn gold.

29 October 2016

The clocks are about to go back. Next week my evening commute will be darker; at 6 p.m. the earth's revolution an hour further onwards than at 6 p.m. today. The rush-hour cars will have their lights on; in towns the terraced rows will glow yellow or flicker with television light. More than at the equinox, it feels to me now that the year has truly turned and there is no longer any denying it. And all over the country, the trees know.

In London streets, parks and gardens they are making themselves ready, the sap retreating and chlorophyll in the leaves breaking down to reveal orange and yellow pigments that have been hidden until now. An abscission layer forms at the leaf stalks, weakening and eventually severing their attachment to the twigs from which, in spring, they grew. Deciduous trees actively shed their leaves in order to weather the winter; gales do not cause, but merely hurry, the process, blanketing gutters and back gardens with arboreal detritus: the untidy makings of future soil.

On Hampstead Heath's western, sandy quarter the silver birch leaves are becoming butter-yellow, though the oaks remain stubbornly emerald with the merest smattering of brown. Beneath them, as the fat acorns fall, grey squirrels are at their most impudent, keeping North London's dogs (and dog walkers) on their toes.

South of the Thames, in Sydenham Hill, one of the last remaining fragments of the ancient Great North Wood is turning golden – with the exception of a few Victorian garden relics like a monkey puzzle and a cedar of Lebanon, both of which will remain dark green year-round. The Nunhead to Crystal Palace railway line once passed through here, and at this time of year bats come together to hibernate in a disused railway tunnel deep in the wood.

All over the city the ash trees are fading elegantly, like aquatints, while rowans on residential pavements proffer bright berries to blackbirds and thrushes, and poplars by the railway lines fling twigs like beckoning fingers down. Here and there a maple flames crimson, while sturdy little hornbeams drop their colour where they stand, leaving a bare tree in a bright puddle – as long as there's no wind.

On wet winter nights in Bloomsbury and Mayfair the London planes under which walked Woolf, Dickens and Orwell still keep watch over the city, their jigsaw bark washed to patchwork richness by the rain.

Another week and another of my neighbours' front gardens is covered over. More and more in the capital have fallen victim to gravel, paving or plain old poured concrete – particularly in areas of high buy-to-let. A couple of semis near me sit behind incongruous forecourts of decorative floor tiles, their gleaming travertine finish a grim prophylactic against nature: here, they seem to declare, nothing living shall ever again appear. Half of London's front gardens have now gone, and there's been a 36 per cent decrease in the last ten years – picture an area two and a half times the size of Hyde Park lost to nature each year.

But the more paving there is in an area the greater the risk of flash flooding; hard surfaces can also create subsidence, interfere with temperature regulation and make a street (and the cars parked on it) dustier and more polluted compared to those lined with plants and grass. But the best reason to keep front gardens alive is for wildlife: everything from rare stag beetles to declining house sparrows, threatened hedgehogs and once-common frogs is being affected by the loss of these little pockets of green.

Although London's crows and magpies are always vocal, and on bright, sunny days you might hear a dunnock or a great tit's repetitive call, there isn't a great deal of proper musical birdsong in autumn and winter – with the honourable exceptions of robins and wrens.

Both male and female robins sing to defend territories, which they hold all year instead of flocking together in winter as many other species do. Some people believe that robins' cold-weather song sounds thinner and somehow more wistful than their fuller spring note; Emily Brontë called it 'wildly tender', which is exactly right.

Given that the wren is one of our tiniest birds (imagine a walnut with an up-cocked tail), its jubilant song is almost improbably loud; in fact, it can carry for up to one kilometre. They're Britain's most numerous breeding bird, but while their size and circumspection means you won't often see one, tune your ears to that rapid-fire trill and you'll find they're everywhere.

Wrens' high metabolic rate means they can be hit hard by harsh winters, so they sometimes tuck themselves up together at night for warmth. Sixty were recorded emerging from one Norfolk nest box: a testament to the tolerance of this otherwise rather solitary bird.

3 December 2016

Everyone I know is hoping for a big waxwing winter. 'What's the weather looking like in Scandinavia,' my birder friends are wondering, 'and what sort of berry crop have they had this year?'

The waxwing is a winter visitor to these isles, a striking, punky bird with a martial crest, Zorro-style eye mask, scarlet buttons and bright-yellow epaulettes on its wings and tail. The species we generally see here is the Bohemian waxwing, named, some say, for its habit of moving around itinerantly in search of food rather than establishing a home territory and staying put; for this reason they don't have a complex territorial song, as (for instance) blackbirds and robins do, but a simple, trilling contact call instead.

Waxwings eat haws, rowan berries and other fruit, feeding cooperatively in sociable flocks; in flight, their triangular

wings can make them look a little like starlings, though
the sound of a flock is very different. Every October and
November some arrive in the north-east of Scotland and
along the east coast of England; but in a 'waxwing winter', triggered by harsh Scandinavian weather or a lack of
food, we're treated to a true irruption as big flocks push far
inland and move south, plundering berry-laden pyracan-
thas in supermarket car parks, congregating in kerbside
rowans and back-garden cotoneasters, and foraging along
farmland hedgerows for sloes and crab apples. To further
please birdwatchers, they tend, while feeding, to show little
fear of humans (they are 'confiding', in twitching lingo),
perching happily for photos against blue, wintry skies.

The British Trust for Ornithology's migration blog
shows a reporting rate well above average for November,
with sightings trackable on Twitter at @WaxwingsUK. I'm
very much your amateur back-garden birdwatcher rather
than someone who'll travel for a tick, so the last time I saw
any was in the winter of 2012–13, when a small raiding party
congregated on Tooting Common for nearly a week. But
those few days really gave me the waxwing bug: a thrilling
mixture of knowing how far these brightly coloured birds
had flown to visit the place where I walked my dog, and not
knowing when they would ever come back.

The ivy has finished flowering, even the huge late-
blooming clump muffling a gatepost two streets from my
house that remained abuzz with insects into the third week

of November. Every time I passed, it announced itself by
its fragrance: sweet, and with overtones that to me suggest
the animal-fat odour of butchers' shops, but which some
have compared to semen. Either way, I'm always surprised
to see 'English Ivy' among the perfumes offered by old-
fashioned toiletry manufacturers.

Ivy isn't a parasite and only uses trees or other structures
for support; but while it doesn't take nutrients from trees
– or 'strangle' them, as people used to think – a really large
burden of ivy can make them more vulnerable in winter to
gales, the evergreen ivy acting like a sail. Only mature ivies
bear flowers and berries; this secondary, 'arboreal' stage is
also marked by the loss of the lobes in their leaves, which
become heart-shaped or oval instead.

As well as supplying vital late-season food for birds, bees
and other insects, ivy makes good cattle fodder and creates
cover for birds and bats, providing them with somewhere
safe and frost-free on winter nights.

We may have had our first real cold snap of the season,
but mild weather earlier in the autumn led to hedgehogs
breeding later, resulting in young too small to survive their
winter hibernation. Wildlife rescue centres across the UK
have reported a spike in underweight hogs needing help.

It's not good news. When I was young, hedgehogs were
widespread: they shuffled about in our garden at dusk, and
as a teenager my husband would walk home from the pub
on spring nights surrounded by the squeaks of courting

males. But their decline since then has been catastrophic, and far from being a common childhood sight most kids now will grow up knowing these charming little creatures only from TV. Their plight throws a stark light on the bio-diversity crash that's occurred in our lifetimes: no longer theoretical, but a creature most of us like and have taken for granted, now largely absent from the lived experience of the generations following ours.

But all is not yet lost. Across the UK over forty thousand people have signed up at www.hedgehogstreet.org to champion their slug-munching garden visitors, giving them access through fences, putting out food and ensuring they have somewhere to hibernate. If you have hogs in your area, consider recruiting your neighbours to their cause, so that when they emerge in spring it is to a hedgehog-friendly world.

7 January 2017

Fog on Wimbledon Common, obscuring the paths, closing down all views and settling among the naked trees like smoke. Fog that jewelled the spider's webs and dampened the skin, rendering the common's familiar acres almost unrecognisable, its spinneys of tall silver birches ghostly and still.

We were there with Scout to walk off some of the Christmas excess. We weren't the only ones, but in the fog, people and dogs loomed suddenly, then just as suddenly disappeared. Sound was dampened, muffled; the place felt eerie and desolate. And then, from somewhere deep in the shrouded woods, a blithe song, the sound of summer, rang out again, and again, and again.

Like most birds bar the robin, song thrushes are usually heard in early summer when they're breeding and defending territories; in fact, their song is the soundtrack of the warmer months in the countryside. They tend to repeat each lilting phrase three, four or five times, then pause, try a new phrase, and so on; this habit makes their song one of the easiest to recognise of all our birds. But every so often one will sing in the depths of winter – perhaps to defend a berry-laden tree – and to hear its note, the essence of summer, when all the world is chill and dark evokes a strange kind of cognitive dissonance.

Both the song thrush and its cousin, the mistle thrush, love snails, bashing them open on stones they use as anvils. Both have beautifully speckled breasts, but the larger and scarcer mistle thrush's song is more like the blackbird's and its alarm call a startlingly loud churr like an old-fashioned wooden football rattle, emitted as it flies. It is the song thrush that is the subject of Thomas Hardy's haunting poem 'The Darkling Thrush', its 'full-hearted evensong / Of joy illimited' ringing out 'When Frost was spectre-grey, / And Winter's dregs made desolate / The weakening eye of day'.

We stood a while and listened, and when we moved on I felt as though the pivot of the year had passed, and spring was – however distantly – on its way.

*

For the last five years, between January 1st and 4th, people across the UK have taken part in the Botanical Society of Britain and Ireland's New Year Plant Hunt, heading out for three hours to their local area to record any wild or naturalised plants that are in bloom. Last year 653 species were identified, making up just over a quarter of the species that occur regularly in Britain and Ireland; there were more blooms in urban areas, which often tend to be warmer and more sheltered, and where more garden escapees are found. Most were hardy weeds that can flower more or less all the time, like dandelions and daisies, or late-blooming plants that had taken advantage of the mild autumn to keep on flowering. Less than 20 per cent of the records were of spring flowers blooming early; it will be fascinating to see if this changes as time goes on and more New Year records are built up. Follow @BSBIbotany on Twitter or go to bsbi.org/new-year-plant-hunt to see the data coming in.

Rarely is my garden without a grey squirrel. They bounce along fences, flicking their tails and goading poor Scout; they dig in my tubs and planters and chase one another dementedly around the lawn. They stripped the wire from our first bird feeder, so we bought one with a protective cage; one got inside it, ate too much and became trapped. Now we have a seed feeder with a spring mechanism that closes the ports to repel boarders; it works, but our new nyger feeder, for the goldfinches, was last week taken apart. Having watched a squirrel a few streets away lugging a whole pain au chocolat up a tree, I'd assumed they wouldn't be interested in tiny nyger seeds. I was wrong.

Grey squirrels excite strong feelings in many, which should come as no surprise. They're a highly assertive, overabundant animal responsible for the decline of native species, and they can cause serious environmental damage. They're also clever, resilient and highly adaptable: a lot like humans, in fact.

11 February 2017

Having done a bunk, as they always do, during the RSPB's annual Big Garden Birdwatch, my feathered friends are back. As I write, a couple of house sparrows are squabbling over our seed feeder as several more sit in the berberis and plot to take their place, while above them in the damson tree a pair of blue tits hopefully await their turn. A female blackbird diligently turns over dead leaves by the shed, while from somewhere in the garden I can hear a great tit calling, a note that will continue until around the end of June.

None of these birds are rare, though many are declining – and neither are the pair of feisty robins, the wood pigeons and dunnocks, the wrens, the voluble magpies, the coal tits and long-tailed tits and goldfinches; nor even the great spotted woodpecker that occasionally investigates the sycamores, or the hulking, golden-eyed sparrowhawk whose aerial beat we're on. None would quicken the heart of an obsessive twitcher; none are the 'charismatic species' beloved of conservationists. But to me they are infinitely precious, their fleeting presence in my urban garden never less than a gift: winged emissaries of wildness, beautiful and perfect, their tolerance of our proximity a more than just reward for the money we spend on seed.

For it can't be easy. Not only must they contend with concrete, cats and garden chemicals, but the same levels of toxic airborne pollution that led in recent weeks to the city's schoolchildren being kept indoors. Birds inhale far more particulates than we do, while prolonged exposure to nitrogen oxides and polycyclic aromatic hydrocarbons (PAHs) have been shown to reduce growth and interfere with egg-laying and brood success, lead to lung damage, lower red blood counts, DNA mutations and cancer. In 1986, birds began to fall dead from the polluted sky above Mexico City; London must clean up its act before ours become canaries in a very densely populated mine.

In the corner of my local park the first arum leaves have appeared. Known as lords-and-ladies, cuckoo pint, adder's root and many other folk names, *Arum maculatum*'s mottled leaves arise from a large, starchy tuber, deep underground, followed in April (hence the 'cuckoo' part of its name, as in cuckoo-spit and cuckoo flower) by a purplish spadix within a sheath, or hood. The odour of the spadix, and its temperature – up to fifteen degrees warmer than the surrounding air – attract insects, which the plant briefly traps and dusts with pollen. 'Pint', which should rhyme with 'mint', derives from 'pintle', or penis, and in some parts of England girls were told as recently as the 1930s not to touch the plant in case it made them pregnant.

In autumn a cluster of orange-red berries is all that remains above ground, held aloft on an erect stalk. While arum berries are poisonous, their nasty taste and the burning sensation they produce in the mouth mean you'd be extremely hard-pressed to eat enough to cause harm.

These are quiet months for lepidopterists. Not a great deal is on the wing bar the winter moth and early moth, succeeded by the spring usher in late February. The females of all three have evolved to become flightless, as is common in winter-active species; this lets them divert scarce energy resources towards producing eggs in time for their caterpillars to feed on the earliest shoots and leaves and, in turn, become the chief food source on which birds like great tits will feed their young.

The names of these three species are rather prosaic, but a great number of our moths, like our fungi, have absolutely spectacular monikers. This is because many did not have common names when they were identified by excitable eighteenth-century naturalists; and since then those names have not been frequently enough used by the general population to have had their fanciful edges smoothed off, forming, instead, the linguistic equivalent of an oxbow lake. And so we have the cloaked carpet and the pinion-spotted pug; the dingy footman and the Hebrew character; the sprawler, the smoky wainscot and the neglected rustic; and surely the most evocative of all: the uncertain.

18 March 2017

What an extraordinary time of year this is. Whenever I step outside it seems something new is happening: bird cherries breaking out in a froth of fresh green leaves; crocuses opening bright gapes to the blue sky; blackbirds, long silent, now in glorious voice. It's the oldest story: the earth coming back to life after its long winter sleep. Yet spring always feels like a miracle when at last it arrives.

I'm listening out for my first chiffchaff of 2017. These khaki-coloured warblers are the first of our summer visitors to arrive, although more and more of them over-winter here these days. Their song is unremarkable – a dull *dink-dink-dink-dink* like a tiny hammer striking an anvil – but hearing it is one of the milestones of my year. It's a way of locating myself in the seasons and staying connected to the natural world – something city living can make more challenging, but which brings tangible benefits for urbanites, I believe.

My efforts are being hampered by a local great tit that's been mustering up a pretty decent impression of a chiff-chaff; in fact, I've had to get my binoculars on the little blighter to be sure. When I began to teach myself birdsong there were two summers when I couldn't reliably hear the difference between a chiffchaff's song and the most monotone of the great tit's extensive repertoire; but I persisted, and at last it clicked. I'm not thrilled to have the waters muddied by a mimic again.

Many of our songbirds copy the songs and calls of other species – and sometimes car alarms, phone ringtones and other sounds too. Studies suggest that doing an impression of other birds can help keep them at bay and so reduce competition for food; a multifarious song has also been shown to boost breeding success in some species, perhaps by demonstrating how worldly-wise and well-travelled a suitor is. For a bird, living long enough to amass a lot of life experiences is proof positive of good genes.

I saw my first butterfly of the year this week: a small tortoiseshell flitting fast and low on Tooting Common in dappled spring sunshine under the oaks. It was a heart-lifting sight.

The small tortoiseshell is often one of the first butterflies out and about in spring as it hibernates over winter, like the peacock, comma and brimstone, rather than spending the colder months as a caterpillar or pupa. That means that as soon as the weather turns warm it's ready to take advantage of early sources of nectar such as forsythia, cherry blossom, mahonia, and the daisies that have this week reappeared on the common, glinting modestly amid the new grass.

The food source for small tortoiseshell caterpillars is the nettle, which is relied on by over forty insect species, including several other butterflies and moths. Thankfully, growing numbers of parks managers and gardeners now appreciate nettles' vital importance and have stopped trying to eradicate them. Even a single trough or tub of them in a corner of your garden can help.

Spring is mostly about beginnings, but it's also a season of endings too. While walking Scout before bed this week I heard the high calls of redwings flying over South London in the dark, and the British Trust for Ornithology's migration blog (www.bto.org/community/bto-blog) confirms that large flocks of them were indeed on the move that night.

Redwings arrive here in autumn, along with fieldfares, waxwings, bramblings and other birds from Scandinavia and Eastern Europe who spend a few brief months with us to escape bitter conditions further north. Their departure signals the end of winter, just as the final sloes, haws and rowan berries have at last been eaten or have shrivelled on the branch.

During the course of this week, an ash tree I pass every day has lost the last of its dangling bunches of seeds, or 'keys'. On the same twigs, black buds are now bursting into exuberant clusters of frilly purple flowers. Out with the old, they declare. Spring is here.

22 April 2017

It's breeding season, and after several years without any nests a pair of blue tits have moved into one of our boxes. They're still at the building stage, the female carrying in scraps of moss, the male shadowing her; I'm waiting for the day she disappears, at which point I'll know she's incubating the eggs – usually eight to ten, and possibly making up more than her own body weight. When the chicks hatch after a couple of weeks the adults will pick up the pace; they'll both be in and out every few seconds, bearing caterpillars, until the nestlings fledge.

I love having a nest in the garden and always feel protective of the baby birds. A few years back two great tits raised a brood in another of our boxes, and I calculated when they would fledge, mindful of cats and the sparrowhawk whose beat our garden is on. On the allotted day I stationed myself in a garden chair with binoculars and a water pistol. I'm proud to say they all survived.

The instinct to identify with and protect 'our' local birds and wildlife is natural; indeed, conservation relies on that sense of stewardship. But like all instincts, it's worth querying. I once stayed in a B&B that had two Larsen traps on its lawn, the owner determined to protect 'her' garden birds. Each metal cage held a live magpie whose job it was to entrap more of its kind so they could be killed.

In a domestic setting, a decision had been made to harm one native species to protect another, the roles of goodie and baddie immutably assigned. The owner knew she wouldn't have any real impact on local magpie numbers; it was about protecting the individual birds she had developed a relationship with. It may not have been rational – for one thing, magpies aren't the only nest predators – but so few of our attitudes to animals, including my own, really are.

Every April the European white elms on my local common are festooned with fat clusters of green seeds. Also known as fluttering elms for the way their lacy, long-stalked flowers dangle in the breeze, they are handsome trees with a large, dense leaf dome, fissured bark and the genus's characteristic asymmetric leaf base.

European white elms aren't resistant to Dutch elm disease, but rarely seem to become infected nonetheless. They're also tolerant of air pollution, flooding and compacted soil. The tallest one on the common, mentioned due to its rarity in several historical tree catalogues and lists, was probably planted as an ornamental; the others, which are some distance away, could well have grown from seed. This species, which can change sex from male to female, is prone to self-pollination, and its seeds are highly viable.

And it's the samaras, or seed casings, that I love elms for. Papery, elegant little discs, in a chic colour combination of chartreuse with magenta hearts, they decorate the spring branches and dress the ground below.

*

I spent a rewarding couple of hours this week helping tidy up a scrap of urban woodland so that it can be used by local children. Knight's Hill Wood is a fragment of the Great North Wood that once covered parts of South London, and which persists in the name of the local area: Norwood. A deodar and Weymouth pine survive from its days as part of a Victorian garden, but like many amenity woods in London it had become ivy-clad, dim and unwelcoming, with sycamore saplings and holly making parts impassable. 'Will you charge kids to play here?' asked one curious passer-by; sadly, it's not such a silly question these days.

The work was organised by a local not-for-profit called Nature Vibezzz. They run free forest school activities for urban kids who might not otherwise have much contact with nature, as well as practical conservancy sessions that connect people to nearby green spaces and improve community cohesion. Time spent in nature benefits children (and adults) in measurable ways, and is vital if we want the next generation to care about and protect our wildlife. There'll be forest school providers, charities and friends organisations doing similar work near you. Seek them out and volunteer, if you can.

27 May 2017

Over Blencathra in the Lake District a small bird of prey was hunting on pointed, backswept wings. Probably a merlin, its shadow moved over the skylarks and meadow pipits nesting on the tussocky slope below.

How much more elegant a sentence it would have made (and how much more expert I would have sounded) if I had simply called it a merlin, and removed the element of doubt. Yet that wouldn't have been true to what happened, because on the hill's flank, the bird distant and in silhouette, I wasn't 100 per cent sure. Raptor ID is tricky for many of us, especially when the bird in question isn't one of the 'big four' (buzzard, sparrowhawk, kestrel, red kite) we often see from the car.

But while wildlife identification brings richness and particularity to the world, wonder happens with or without it. We should never let taxonomy be a barrier to engagement; this beautiful apex predator was thrilling, merlin or not.

A few days later, climbing Helvellyn with my husband, there were two smart wheatears (or white-arses, to give them their old, unbowdlerized moniker), a lark playing tiny aerial bagpipes, and several more meadow pipits on the scree slopes. Dubbed 'mipits' by birders, both for ease and to show you're 'in the know', these modest brown birds' calls are the soundtrack to moorland hikes.

But there should have been greater numbers, and more variety. That we're missing birds from these denuded habitats is undeniable, with more and more upland species red-listed; what's harder is turning things around. Powerful stakeholders, from conservation bodies and landowners to farmers and field sports organisations, are vying both to divest themselves of blame and to claim sole ownership of the solution. All boast differing expertise and a range of justly passionate voices; but on the sidelines strident journalists of all stripes muddy the waters while an army of online tribalists take potshots at one another, their point-scoring only deepening mistrust and entrenching the divide.

Respectful dialogue is the only way forward – perhaps out of view of those for whom compromise is anathema. Meanwhile, amid the mud-slinging, upland-loving birds like the whinchat, dotterel and curlew fade quietly – and heartbreakingly – from view.

Here and there amid the uniform green of so-called 'improved' pasture, Cumbria's last traditional hay meadows are coming into bloom, their grass mingled richly with bright buttercups, ribwort plantain, red campion, scabious, pignut, clover, speedwell, lesser stitchwort and dozens of other wildflowers, at an astonishing density of up to fifty species per square metre.

There are thought to be fewer than ten thousand hectares of old-fashioned hay meadow left in Britain, perhaps only one thousand in upland areas, with 97 per cent lost between the 1930s and 1980s due to agricultural intensification. Their diversity, established over centuries, provides a far better habitat than modern, monoculture grass leys. Hay meadows can support up to a tonne of bees, butterflies and other insects per five acres, as well as voles, shrews, slow worms and lizards, and many seed-eating and ground-nesting birds. Further up the food chain, there are foxes, stoats and kestrels, swallows hawking for crane flies, and barn owls that emerge at dusk to hunt voles.

Hay from traditionally managed, wildflower-rich meadows is also an impressive source of sugars and minerals. One Herefordshire site I know of sells theirs to feed racehorses, and when the aftermath is grazed, the sheep ignore their bucket mineral licks as the deeper-rooted plants amid the grasses draw everything they need up from underground.

'Oak before ash, we're in for a splash; ash before oak, we're in for a soak' – or so the saying goes. But surely the rhyme is descriptive rather than predictive, the relative leafing of the two trees an indication of the preceding atmospheric conditions, rather than those to come.

Certainly, the ash trees here in Cumbria are weeks behind the oaks. That's no surprise, as ashes are much more shallow-rooted than oaks with their deep tap roots. It's been a dry winter, and a dry spring too, and while oaks have been able to draw up enough water to produce their leaves, the ash trees, rooted in drier surface soil, have had far less to work with. No wonder from a distance many here look almost dead beside their lushly leafed companions: bedecked with last year's susurrating ash keys, but their down-beckoning twigs barely even breaking into bud.

1 July 2017

It's coming up to two months since swifts arrived back in our summer skies, screaming in from Africa in the first week of May like squadrons of joyful, black-feathered Exocets. Now this year's youngsters are due to fledge, dropping out of their nests in the eaves of tall buildings into limitless skies. Imagine it: years spent in flight, crossing and recrossing continents and never touching the ground, living in the air as a fish lives in water. They are utterly extraordinary birds.

Many people find it difficult to tell the difference between swifts, swallows and house martins, but once you get your eye (and ear) in, the difference is clear. Swifts' long wings are recurved, giving them a distinct crescent-shaped silhouette, and they appear all black, lacking the pale tummies of house martins and swallows; their high-pitched screams are also unmistakable: 'such an expression of pent-up joy as little children would make if unexpectedly released from school, furnished with wings, and flung up into the air for a game of hide-and-seek among the clouds', wrote the Revd C. A. Johns.

I contacted people responsible for both the buildings near me where swifts nest. One, a church, has a new roof complete with impenetrable soffits; the other, a block of flats, has replaced the ventilation bricks swifts used for access – they were letting in water, the contractor said, though as the holes were angled downwards I couldn't see how. It turns out that neither site has replaced the habitat they destroyed with nest boxes or swift bricks.

Swifts are extremely site-faithful, and when I saw them return at the start of May I hoped against hope that they would find a nook or ledge somewhere close by. Sadly, it doesn't look as though they have managed to, and sitting in my garden in the hot weather this June there were, for the first time in twelve years, no swifts screaming joyfully in the skies overhead.*

It's National Meadows Day today, and while you could be forgiven for wondering whether there's anything left at all that doesn't have its own 'day', I rather like the idea of drawing Britain's meadows to our collective attention on 1 July each year. For what could be more wonderful than a field of tall summer grass, swaying in the wind, alive with butterflies and studded with orchids and other wildflowers?

Since the Second World War, hay meadows' ancient, species-rich tapestries have been replaced with reliable, 'weed'-free grass leys suitable for the production of silage. With them we've seen the loss or steep decline of many of our most iconic species, including corncrakes, harvest mice and glow-worms.

This year, the charity People Need Nature has created a soundscape celebrating Britain's lost wildflower meadows.

---

* When the Swift Mapper app was released in 2020 by RSPB, Swift Conservation, Action for Swifts and Swifts Local Network, data suggested that both nest sites have indeed been destroyed.

It can be streamed or downloaded free from peopleneed nature.org.uk, and is a gorgeously rich and evocative reminder of why we must protect the meadows we have left.

The recent fine weather was good for butterflies, and this week I've spotted red admirals, large skippers and ringlets along with the speckled woods and holly blues I more usually see; while watering the garden one evening I also disturbed a lovely yellow brimstone moth that had been sheltering in my laurel. Disappointingly, though, no hawkmoths yet.

But there should be far more. Michael McCarthy's sobering and inspiring book *The Moth Snowstorm: Nature and Joy* really brings home the lost abundance of Britain's invertebrates during our lifetimes, and it is shocking; even more so when one considers their foundational role in the food pyramid and how much else depends on them.

But there is hope. The fact that there are butterflies at all on Tooting Common – and grasshoppers and crickets, stag beetles and moths – is testament to an enlightened management programme that leaves areas of vegetation uncut and unsprayed: big banks of brambles and nettles, dead wood left to rot, and unmown grass; it's something we can all replicate in our gardens, and press our councils to emulate. 'Let them be left, O let them be left,' wrote Gerard Manley Hopkins, presciently; 'Long live the weeds and the wilderness yet.'

5 August 2017

You can feel it, can't you: the moment the year turns, usually in late July. Somewhere between spring's last blackbird recital and the first of the swifts to slip away south comes a day when all the mad uprush of growth and procreation, having slowed, simply halts. Then for a while the summer rests in fullness, like a held breath, before the living world falls gradually back into senescence again.

We have passed that tipping point, which is not to say there's no summer still to come – though warm weather's far from guaranteed. But for the most part, and excepting non-native garden plants imported for late-summer colour, the natural world has passed its yearly peak. Most birds have bred; the trees' leaves, all now out, will toughen and darken; energy will be diverted from vegetal growth to the setting of fruits, nuts and seeds, and even the nettles will lose vigour, and their sting.

One non-native now entering its blooming period is Himalayan balsam or kiss-me-on-the-mountain, a tall, pink-flowered relative of pub window box favourite the busy Lizzie. Himalayan balsam escaped from gardens after being introduced as an ornamental by Victorian botanists in 1839 and has since become a naturalised annual weed, flourishing particularly on riverbanks, where it forms dense thickets and chokes off other vegetation important for native plants and animals. Worse, when it dies off in winter, it leaves long stretches of bank completely bare and vulnerable to erosion.

Control of Himalayan balsam must be carried out before it sets seed, and 'balsam-bashing' volunteer days are not uncommon in affected areas. But in Hertfordshire, one distillery has partnered with its local Wildlife Trust to harvest it carefully while in early flower and make a pink tipple from the dried blooms instead. For each bottle of Puddingstone Distillery's Campfire Gin Special Edition No 1, £2 goes to Herts and Middlesex Wildlife Trust.

The blackberries are early this year, and the bramble banks on Tooting Common are covered in fat, ripe berries. But what variety they are I couldn't say.

There are over 320 microspecies of bramble in the British Isles, their diversity a result of their complex reproductive habits: not only are some plants polyploids (having double or treble the usual number of chromosomes) but the formation of fruits can occur both sexually or by apomixis, a highly efficient form of asexual reproduction without fertilisation.

The study of brambles is known as batology, and while perhaps something of a niche field it's a specialism highly prized in forensic botany. Because brambles have a fast and highly consistent growth pattern, a batologist can date a crime scene with astonishing accuracy by examining the spread of brambles across the site.

Watching my husband haul a nineteen-kilogram 'rocket log' (a single-log bonfire) a kilometre or more across a muddy, rain-swept Cornish field last weekend, I had good cause – and ample time – to ponder our wisdom in purchasing such a thing. Port Eliot Festival is magical in sunny weather, a little less so in a biblical downpour; what it definitely didn't need was the added challenge of a caber toss.

At least our money went to a good cause: the Hillyfield is a small, sustainably managed wood on Dartmoor, a real beacon when it comes to community engagement, heritage crafts and ecological regeneration. Bafflingly, its continued existence is threatened by no less a body than the Dartmoor National Park, whose objection to owner Doug King-Smith's need for on-site infrastructure such as a wood-drying barn has led it into a strange position seemingly at odds with its own stated aims. A public inquiry will decide, with King-Smith forced to crowdfund his legal costs, so I'm glad to have contributed my money – if not my muscle.* Looking back, though, we probably should have purchased something portable from the Hillyfield stand, like a nice trio of treen bowls, instead.

21 October 2017

What heart-stopping creatures birds of prey are, and how extraordinary it feels to see one deep in the heart of the city. There's a strange cognitive dissonance about such beautiful wild creatures deigning to occupy a habitat so altered

---

* The inquiry was held in April 2018 and an agreement reached between Hillyfield and the Dartmoor National Park Authority.

by humans, one in which traffic snarls, fumes rise and the tilting landscape below them must appear, in places, just a grid of roads and steel and glass.

I've had two brushes with raptors in recent weeks, and both left me exhilarated and grinning, transported entirely out of my London life. In the first, I was curled up on my sofa with my laptop, French doors open to my scrappy garden, when my local sparrows began to make a racket in the thorny berberis by the fence. They do this often, and usually it's what's coyly known as a 'sparrow wedding', but the tenor seemed more belligerent than usual so I went to take a look. As I did, a male sparrowhawk broke from deep in the berberis just a few feet away and flew to the ridge of my neighbour's roof, where he perched for a moment, flustered and outraged. A pair of 'sprawks' nested on Tooting Common this summer, and my local bird recorder, Peter White, reports that all five chicks successfully fledged, so my backyard visitor could well have been one of them; certainly, it looked as though he needed to practise his skills.

And then, this week, I was playing fetch with Scout on the common before work when I heard an unfamiliar bird calling repeatedly from somewhere close by. A raptor was flying low, in loose circles, around the grassy area: slim and elegant, with a long tail and strikingly backswept wings. It was a juvenile hobby: lovely little predators fast enough to seize swifts in flight and nimble enough to catch dragonflies on the wing. At this time of year they are leaving us, flying south to sub-Saharan Africa only to return again in spring. The British Trust for Ornithology reports that numbers here are rising, bucking the UK's overall trend for species decline; they've also expanded their range north and west, something that could well be linked to climate change.

The sparrowhawk in the berberis may have been hard to miss, but a few years back I'd never have been able to identify a hobby; in fact, I wouldn't even have registered that there was an unfamiliar bird nearby. It's easy to think that people who know about birds are a separate species themselves: fleece-clad, hung about with binoculars and cameras, and brandishing their 'life lists'. But like anything, learning about birds is a process – one it's never too late to embark on. Apps make it easy to keep an ID guide on you; simple curiosity does the rest. I started small, with the birds in my garden; slowly, more and more species swam out of anonymity into sharp focus, along with their behaviour, their yearly schedules, their songs and calls. The reason I even turned to look at the hobby overhead was that my brain no longer relegates bird calls to background noise. This is a change anyone can make.

Why would you want to, though – why make room, when there are so many other things claiming our time? Because the things we choose to look at in life loom large, changing the version of reality we live in, whether it's cars or fashion or the natural world. Knowing one bird from another tells me how many different species are around me, populating my urban world with their lives; learning about trees has made my city seem greener, because my eye no longer passes over them as though they were hardly there. If you live in a city and miss 'nature', the answer doesn't have to be to move out; it's to tune in.

A friend of mine who works in reptile conservation posted a photograph on social media recently of a juvenile grass snake coiling around his finger, its head back, mouth open, playing dead – a common response. The tiny snake was utterly beautiful: new-minted and glossy. Yet among the admiring responses were a couple objecting to the depiction of an animal 'in distress'. My friend was accused of cruelty, and I of retweeting an image in poor taste.

This kind of piousness seems to be everywhere at the moment, and as a distorted, purist exaggeration of the general message to care for the environment it risks impinging on our ability to interact with nature in any meaningful way. Of course it's wrong to collect birds' eggs now that so many species are in decline, and the nasty trend for releasing butterflies at weddings should be discouraged; but if kids aren't allowed to pick common wildflowers, pebbles can no longer be taken from beaches and naturalists can't handle the creatures they're studying we may as well give up on relating to anything at all beyond our screens.

18 November 2017

In November the sky can be slate-grey and sullen; high, blue and equinoctial; or illumined by low, lemony winter light. As the leaves fall, black branches jut across it like a woodcut, and fistfuls of birds are flung overhead.

Now is the time to look out for birds flocking, whether it's murmurations of starlings, wintering waders at the shoreline, rooks and jackdaws over woodland or long, wavering skeins of geese. Finches and tits form mixed flocks in the colder months, while migrant redwings and fieldfares stick together in busy work parties while feeding too. Whatever the day's weather, few things define the season more unambiguously for me than the glimpse of a flock of birds moving from place to place.

The smart little pied wagtail, jaunty and bold in service station car parks or bobbing its long tail beside ditches and streams, is not a bird you might think of in terms of communal behaviour, but in winter they often form nightly roosts several thousand strong. In Dublin city centre over three thousand have been recorded; in some years, two thousand or so sleep in floodlit plane trees between a multi-storey car park and Heathrow's Terminal 5. Rather wonderfully, Berkhamsted had a small roost in the municipal Christmas tree one year where the birds may have benefited from the extra warmth of the decorative lights: wagtails can lose up to 20 per cent of their body weight on a cold night just trying to keep warm.

One of the largest pied wagtail roosts ever recorded was in Orpington, Kent, in a dense group of evergreen laurel bushes between the railway station and Crofton Halls. Once the birds were in they were invisible, and utterly silent; you could have passed within a few feet of them and never known that in the darkness of a November evening over four thousand hearts were beating nervously nearby.

Recent days have brought with them a presage of winter, and the first frost has bletted the fruits on the ornamental quince at the front of my house. Still going strong, though, are the cheerful orange nasturtiums (*Tropaeolum majus*) trumpeting from front gardens up and down my street.

A native of South America – the lower latitude the reason for their later flowering time – nasturtiums' common name comes from Latin *nasus* (nose) and *tortus* (twisted), for the flower shape and the leaves' peppery smell. Why, then, is *Nasturtium officinale* the scientific name of watercress, which, although also edible, is a completely different plant; and why are garden nasturtiums also sometimes known as Indian cress?

To avoid confusion J. R. R. Tolkien preferred 'nasturtian', kicking up a stink after it was 'corrected' in the first print run of volume one of *The Lord of the Rings*. Insisting on its reinstatement, he consulted the gardener at his Oxford college: 'What do you call these things?' 'I calls them *Tropaeolum*, sir.' 'But when you're just talking to dons?' 'I says *nasturtians*, sir.' 'Not *nasturtium*?' 'No, sir; that's watercress.'

'Though I do not much care,' he lied blatantly in a letter a few days after publication, 'I dug my toes in. *Nasturtium* is . . . bogusly botanical, and falsely learned.'

News came this week of seahorses living in the Thames – and not out in its boskier reaches but in the city itself, at Greenwich and the South Bank. Both the short-snouted and the spiny variety turn up in London waters from time to time, but now the Zoological Society of London (ZSL) has confirmed that the river has resident populations of both – and this in one of the busiest urban waterways in the world.

Seahorses are magical little creatures, and importantly they're sticklers for clean water – amazing, given that just sixty years ago the polluted old Thames was found to be functionally dead. Amid the constant flood of bad news about nature and the environment, this is worth taking a moment to contemplate.

We *can* turn things around, and when we do, the natural world is often ready to forgive us. But we have to have hope, and the energy to try. There's clear blue water between the paralysis of despair and Pollyanna-ish naivety, and it's vital that we inhabit it. After all, it's where the urban seahorses live.

COUNTRYSIDE

23 December 2017

For the two decades in which I lived in London I would barely notice the winter solstice, which fell two days ago. The clocks going back in October made a difference to my mornings, and to how dark it was when I left work; but the shortening of the days was offset by street lights, well-lit public transport, and buildings that left their lights on round the clock. The working day was no shorter than in summer; in fact, in the run-up to Christmas the shops stayed open later every night. Nothing slowed, contracted or dimmed to mark the shortest day of the year, for like all megacities London has all but left such trifling considerations behind.

But now I live in Suffolk, in a village entirely without street lights, and the difference could not be more marked. When I wake, at my usual time, the world outside is dim, the yellow windows of nearby farmhouses glimmering beyond frost-white fields. By mid-morning the sun is properly up, and there may even be some winter sunshine for an hour or two; but not long after lunch it's time to complete any outdoor jobs because the light will soon begin to fail. At three o'clock the restless rooks are already gathering in the leafless trees, and flocks of starlings start to move from place to place. When darkness falls, the winter nights are blacker than I've ever seen, with a starfield so breathtaking that on clear nights the familiar configurations of Orion and the Plough are lost amid a million other points of light.

Here the ancient strictures of the seasons still hold sway, and at the winter solstice, when the living world draws in to its coldest, stillest point, there is a primeval kind of comfort to be found in a good torch, a well-stocked pantry and a stack of seasoned wood for the fire.

Carrion crows and magpies are the corvids most famil-iar to city-dwellers, but in Suffolk's arable heartlands it is the rook that is most commonly seen. Similar to crows only superficially, their long grey beak is bare at its base, and they sport thickly feathered 'trousers' that give them a slightly waddling gait as they process across a field inspecting it for grubs. Rooks are also more com-munal in their behaviour, though the old saw 'If there's more than one crow they're rooks, if there's only one rook it's a crow' doesn't hold water, for many places – not least Tooting Common, where I used to walk Scout – have resident populations of crows that feed together all year round.

In *British Birds in Their Haunts* the Revd C. A. Johns writes that the rook is 'everywhere encouraged and indeed all but domesticated. There are few . . . propri-etors of modern demesnes pretending to be parks, who would not purchase at a high price the air of antiquity and respectability connected with an established colony.' He admits that they can decimate young crops, but argues that their good offices in eating wireworms, leatherjackets and other pests more than make up for it.

Johns's entry on rooks runs to several pages, yet he clearly could have written more: 'How the birds squabble about their nests, how they punish those thievishly disposed, how they drive away intruders from strange rookeries . . . how every time that a bird caws while perched he strains his whole body forward and expands his wings with the effort, all these things, and many more, I must pass over without further notice, leaving them to be verified by the reader with the help of a spy-glass, or, what is far better, a good double opera-glass.'

Christmas seems to come around so quickly each year now, with its surfeit of food and festivities, its colours and carols and excess. Winter feasting counteracts the terrifying austerity of the natural world, which in midwinter is, without our modern comforts, a near-unsurvivable place. Yet outside, as we celebrate, the struggle for life goes on unremarked: badgers dig for torpid worms; molehills are thrown up; deer leave their slot-marks in puddle margins and the carolling of wrens sings out the fact of their survival. *Alleluia!* they sing; *psallat iam in lustro*: now sing in brightness. And so they do.

20 January 2018

I got the tip-off from the TV aerial engineer. Having established that I was new to Suffolk, and – given the animal skulls, antlers and feathers in my living room – interested in the natural world, he said, 'Staverton Park: that's where you want to go. Only small, but it's like another world. There's a white deer in there too; I've seen it myself.'

'An awesome place of Tolkienesque wonder and beauty', Oliver Rackham called Staverton Park, or Staverton Thicks, in his seminal *History of the Countryside*. 'The mighty and bizarre shapes of oaks of unknown age rise out of a sea of tall bracken, or else are mysteriously surrounded by rings of yet mightier hollies.'

The oaks' ages are hard to determine as many are pollards, a management technique that both alters trees' girth and height and prolongs their life. I found specimens that it would have taken four people to put their arms around, and some are recorded as having a DBH (diameter at breast height) of well over seven metres. This silent gathering of gnarled sentinels was like an army of Ents: each twisted bole or hollow trunk somehow very much a being, not just a tree.

But what made the wood more extraordinary was the fact that the secondary tree was holly, and not as shrubs or understorey but reaching enormous heights – some well over twenty metres tall, with thick trunks: taller than anywhere else in the UK. In the dim January light the leafless oaks feigned death, but the hollies, leaves smooth with age, were rich green, some dripping with blood-red berries. There was definitely something of the fairy tale about the place, I thought, as I trod softly between the huge trees. Of *course* it would harbour a white hart.

If it was there, I didn't see it; but perhaps it saw me, for the feeling of being watched was intense. Some believe this tiny patch of land to have been continuously forested – albeit by different types of trees – since the Wildwood, and perhaps some ancient part of my brain knew it, for as a modern human I felt small, and comparatively young, and not at all the dominant species there.

January marks the start of the breeding season for brown hares, and although it peaks in March, already I have seen them in the Suffolk fields: racing away from me through the sugar beet, leggy as deer, but also in pairs, feinting a little half-heartedly in the water meadow I can see from my bedroom window.

On a walk, visiting friends have exclaimed, 'Is that a rabbit or a hare?' – but asking the question invariably means it's a rabbit, for a hare is unmistakable. Seen in motion, they are to rabbits as wolves are to King Charles spaniels.

Like many people my age, my fascination with hares was sparked by Kit Williams's 1979 book *Masquerade*, which featured a bejewelled golden hare hidden somewhere in Britain, the clues to its location concealed in fifteen lavish illustrations. The book was merely the latest layer in a long tradition of mythologising, for unlike rabbits, wherever hares occur our forebears have interpreted them as magical or symbolic too.

One of my first purchases, after moving here, was a bird feeder, but it took a little while to find the right spot and for two weeks no birds came. Then I moved it to a fig that grows between mine and my neighbour's front gardens, and within minutes they arrived.

The first to scope it out was a dunnock. Easily mistaken for a sparrow, they have a finer bill, like a robin's, and a sleek grey head. On sunny days I've heard them in the hedges, their strident, scratchy song ringing out repetitively and earning them their other name of hedge accentor. They're mostly insectivorous, but they will eat small seeds, and once he'd got up his courage – dunnocks are quite low in the pecking order – this one certainly did.

In the breeding season dunnocks form complex relationships, some monogamous, some polyandrous or polygynous and some even polygynandrous, meaning a sexual group of several males and several females. Free love: who'd have thought it of such a shy and retiring little bird?

24 February 2018

I met an English elm this week, quite unexpectedly, in a new neighbour's garden. Once so ubiquitous as to be part of the backdrop, by the time I was born, in 1975, Britain's

Ulmus minor 'Atinia' were nearly all dead or dying from Dutch elm disease. When the storm of 1987 took down most of the standing dead wood it erased a native tree from our landscape, something we may now need to brace ourselves for again, with ash dieback disease.

Elms do live on in hedgerows, never reaching the height at which they become vulnerable to attack from the flying beetles carrying fungal spores spelling out their doom; and Brighton has held on to several thousand, protected partly by local efforts and partly by the South Downs. But I was thrilled to find a mature, healthy specimen (touch wood!) in a Suffolk village – and, in a further nod to history, colonised by rooks. There had once been more elms, my neighbour told me, saved by her father from the tree-feller and carefully tended. Sadly, all but one had eventually succumbed to disease.

One of the difficulties conservationists face when trying to rally the public behind a cause is that of 'shifting baselines': our all-too-human belief that the world we inherit is the benchmark from which change deviates, a belief that makes us liable to accept radically degraded landscapes as the norm. What matter that elms are gone, if to those my age and younger the countryside still looks full of stately trees? What matter that there were once so many more birds in Britain if the dawn chorus still sounds sweet to modern ears?

But human lives are short and we take too much for granted, often only valuing nature in terms of its utility to us. We no longer rely on *Fraxinus excelsior* to make furniture or tool handles, and our children may not be able to identify its leaves, but when our ash trees begin to fall unheard in the forests, the sound they make will be one of loss.

The village hedgerows have been flailed and now look stark and smashed, the line left by the tractor's cutter bar brutally exact. It could be worse: it's better to cut in January than in September, for an autumn cut means berries and fruit are lost to overwintering birds and small mammals. And come March it'll be bird-nesting season, when laws come into place to protect breeding habitats.

It's naive to expect farmers to lay hedges in the painstaking traditional manner, or pay for the labour involved in trimming miles of them by hand. But frequent flailing encourages overgrowth at the top while making the base spindly and gappy, stopping it being stockproof and drastically reducing its value to wildlife. The ecologist Miles King calls them 'zombie hedges': they stagger on, wretchedly deformed and shockingly devoid of life.

But perhaps there's a compromise to be reached. A 2015 study by the Centre for Ecology and Hydrology found that cutting once every three years, with the bars set a little higher and wider, dramatically increased hedges' value for wildlife, supporting greater numbers of pollinators, butterflies and moths, and more mammals and farmland birds.

*

It was a clear night, Orion and the Plough blazing out amid a welter of stars invisible in towns and cities. I woke to a white frost that rimed the grass of the water meadows, fog veiling the skeletal crack willows and alders by the stream. And yet it was spring: I heard it in the notes of the wood pigeon croodling from my chimney; I saw it in the way the piebald pony in the nearby paddock ran in joyful circles, kicking up its heels.

By the time I was out with Scout the sun had melted the frost everywhere but in the shadows, so that the shapes of trees reached out whitely across the grass. The hazels were hung with catkins and there were daisies and dog violets on the village verges, and in the spinneys we saw carpets of snowdrops and winter aconites.

And then I heard it: my first blackbird of 2018, and the surest sign of the turning of the year. It'll be a few weeks until they're in full, fluty song, but even so, those familiar notes from deep in a wintry thicket made my spirit soar.

31 March 2018

'Have you seen it yet?' people have been asking me since I moved to Suffolk. 'No? Well, never mind. You will soon, I'm sure.' Each new friend or neighbour, it seems, has had the same question for me, as soon as they learn that I write about nature for a living: 'Have you seen the barn owl yet?'

My cottage looks out over a water meadow home to rabbits, hares, visiting fieldfares, pheasants, rooks and many moles. Bounded on three sides by roads and resown to grass last year, it's not the tall tangle that's best for small mammals like voles, though there are a few straggly ditches lined with crack willows, and some areas of rough grassland nearby. I wouldn't have pegged it as barn owl habitat were it not for the fact that one of the other cottages in my little row is named after them; generations of these beautiful birds, it seems, have made this village their home.

So I've been keeping my binoculars handy just in case, and while washing up I gaze out of the kitchen window, scanning the meadow for that characteristic white shape. I've seen plenty of gulls and sunlit wood pigeons and, once, an egret; but until last week there was no barn owl.

And then one day at just after 5 p.m. there it was, ghosting low up the ditch towards the cottage, making straight for me where I stood in the living room forgetting to breathe. Scrambling for the binoculars, I watched it turn the beautiful heart of its facial disc this way and that; I saw rabbits scurry for cover as it drifted over them, and then it turned at the fence, perhaps fifteen feet from me, to head for the paddock where the horses graze. A few minutes later it swung back around and again quartered the water meadow with soft, slow wingbeats; I watched it, laughing, utterly uplifted. To be able to see hares and barn owls without leaving my house is an astonishing and unlooked-for gift.

*

It was my friend Emma, a botanist and craft writer, who spotted them in the churchyard: a clump of wild daffodils, paler and prettier than the brash yellow trumpets of the supermarket aisles. In the days that followed, my eye in, I found more around the village. Lenten lilies are much rarer than a hundred years ago, but while I've seen them in Cumbria I hadn't expected them here and so my eye had passed over them without properly seeing what they were. For me, taxonomy is less about the ability to categorise and more about separating one thing from another. The world is richer for knowing that there are more things in it, rather than just for being able to label them correctly.

But how hard it is to see daffodils as they must have appeared to our forebears: simply a wild, self-willed spring flower, like our native bluebells, whose mass yearly blooming was worth taking a special trip to see. Our brassy, standardised modern cultivars, municipally planted or barcoded by the tills, are now so ubiquitous as to have become a product divorced, almost, from nature; meanwhile, in our collective imagination, the wild original fades from view.

It was cheering to spot a fat female yellowhammer in a hedge on one of my daily walks around the fields; but then how shocking to see the news, a few days later, of the catastrophic collapse of farmland birds across France, a story that made the front page of *Le Monde*. Many such species in the UK are also in freefall as intensive farming practices and the increased use of pesticides wipe out their habitats and sources of food. The Farmland Bird Index reveals ongoing declines since the 1970s, with a decline of nearly a tenth in the last five years alone.

Our reliance on cheap, unsustainable, intensively produced food has, in the last forty years, caused an ecological catastrophe that may well prove to be irreversible. We urgently need a new agricultural system that supports farmers in protecting the complex web of life on which, ultimately, we all depend. Until then, choosing organic produce or, better still, buying direct from small farmers is perhaps the best thing we as consumers can do.

5 May 2018

For many years, while still living in London, I went on spring pilgrimages to try and hear nightingales; this spring, in Suffolk, one has come to me. I'd set out on a Sunday morning to visit the local bluebell wood, and while walking back to the village heard a distant sound that brought me up short. Almost lost amid the chorus of birdsong was a faint but unmistakable *jug-jug-jug-jug*, and then a repeated, ascending whistle, piercing and sweet.

After some exploration I managed to come within about ten metres of the thicket the song was issuing from, although nightingales are so shy and ventriloquial it can be hard to know exactly where they are. Recently arrived, this male was not quite in full voice, perhaps tired from his long migration; or perhaps he was saving himself for nightfall, when their extraordinary song stands out best.

A recent study found that the song of a male nightingale acts as a highly reliable advertisement of his fitness as a partner. 'Better' singers – measured by metrics such as complexity, order and repetition of song features such as trills, whistles and buzzes – contribute more to chick-feeding; it seems that male nightingales who are all mouth are usually trousers too. Additionally, the orderliness of the song increases in individuals with age, perhaps serving as an indication to potential mates that with age comes wisdom – or at least, knowledge of where the safest nest sites and richest food sources are to be found.

Hearing a nightingale sing is like briefly falling in love, so utterly intense an experience it is; given their rapid decline it also provokes the same half-stifled sense of precariousness and loss. When at last I managed to tear myself away – joy-struck, heartsore, flooded with feeling – everything around me appeared even more beautiful than it had before.

As I passed our little village church the sound of morning service reached me, but I felt blessed by my encounter with the nightingale. My own holy communion had already taken place.

By the time I saw my first swallow of the year I was starting to become anxious. They weren't late by my old London standards, but I'd expected to see one in Suffolk several days before they'd normally appear over the Smoke. I fitted a hirundine nest cup to the eaves of my cottage, and as the weather warmed I scanned the skies. But no swallows appeared, and a friend in the South of France tweeted to say that she hadn't seen any either. I began to worry about what might have happened to the tiny eighteen-gram birds on their six-thousand-mile trip.

And then at last there they were over the paddock, sleek, ebullient and so instantly familiar it was as though they had never left our skies. Yet something in the intensity of the relief I felt at their return gave me pause.

These are unsettled times, acute geopolitical tensions playing out against a backdrop of devastating environmental loss. Small wonder that we need the reassurance of the circling seasons and their natural markers, like swallows; the question is, for how much longer can we keep expecting the natural world to bounce back?

Many of the garden weeds in Suffolk differ from those in London, and in place of ugly annual mercury my beds here are smothered in garlic mustard instead. It's a crucial food plant for the caterpillars of orange-tips, so instead of pulling it all out I'm leaving it to flourish here and there. I've also moved some nettles – great for several species of butterfly – to a sunny spot at the back of the garden, and am introducing to my lawn some smaller, nectar- and pollen-rich wildflowers that more traditional gardeners might call weeds.

The culprit is a book by garden writer Kate Bradbury called *The Bumblebee Flies Anyway*. Her vision of a garden as an ecosystem humming with life, its owner as proud creator and custodian, is so beguiling it's utterly overhauled whatever previous conceptions I had. Surely the best measure of success is the contribution your home patch makes to conserving the nation's biodiversity, not the neatness of your lawn's edges or how many exotic cultivars you boast.

9 June 2018

When I am in the countryside, London seems unimaginable: its noise and fumes, its hardness and unrelenting pace. But when I'm working in London it's Suffolk's lushness I can't picture. Waiting for a bus on the busy Hackney Road, the village I spend most of the month in seems an entirely impossible place.

Yet spring has transformed both places so thoroughly that now it's winter that seems the greatest improbability of all. In May I watched as one East London park became a mass of bird cherry blossom, the trees' fragrant, creamy-white racemes turning each tarmac path into a bridal aisle for commuters and a banquet for pollinators, drifts of petals collecting in the grimy gutters like snow. As I passed through every morning I heard the spring carolling of blackbirds from the trees – just as my Suffolk blackbird was probably singing from the clay pantiles of the little rented cottage that's now home. Trees and birds, blossom and bees: spring exerts its generative pull on all the natural world, regardless of town or countryside.

There were great tits calling insistently on Pentonville Road, and pied wagtails flirting their tails on the sun-warmed slate roofs of Islington office blocks. One morning during rush hour, not far from BBC Broadcasting House, I heard a robin spilling out its bright lament. And everywhere, weeds and wildflowers were making a dash for it: greening pavement cracks and crevices, crowding around the roots of street trees and shooting up on scrappy verges, reaching for the sun.

If you live and work in a city, it's easy to miss spring. The sun shines more reliably, and the temperatures rise, but the lushness and growth – the sense of it as a period of mad, unfettered reproduction – can pass you by. It's everywhere, though, if you can only tune in to its frequency. Even above the steel and glass towers of Old Street roundabout wheel the migratory swifts.

Bethnal Green seems an unlikely place to see a butterfly, yet there one was, dancing down a busy side road flanked by parked cars and, beyond them, high-rise flats. I could tell from its size and style of flight that it was a skipper, a group of primitive butterflies with short wings and fat bodies that make them almost seem more like moths. They're well named, flying fast and apparently skittishly – though amid tall grass their deft manoeuvrability becomes clear. Rusty orange, the one I saw was probably a small skipper or an Essex skipper; only a close look at its antennae could have told me for sure.

Last month forty-two of their cousins the chequered skippers, extinct in England since 1976, were released in Rockingham Forest in Northamptonshire as part of the National Lottery Heritage Fund's Back From the Brink project. Brought here from Belgium, many of the females were carrying eggs, and it's hoped that with careful management of the release site they may eventually recolonise the country – just as has happened with red kites.

Today marks the start of Cherishing Churchyards Week, an initiative set up by environmental charity Caring for God's Acre, of which HRH the Prince of Wales is president. Britain's twenty thousand burial grounds are fantastic for nature, having largely escaped chemicals and cultivation. In my local Suffolk churchyard, meadow saxifrage, in steep decline nationally, still blooms among the graves.

In cities, burial grounds are particularly vital, as green spaces can be in short supply. So I was concerned to learn of the work being carried out at Camberwell Cemeteries in South London, a once-beautiful site where plans to create 4,865 more plots have led to the felling of hundreds of mature trees, wildlife-rich scrub being cleared and the loss of acres of meadow habitat – not to mention some headstones, memorials, and unmarked paupers' graves.

We, the living, need nature – and not as some kind of luxury or afterthought: trees and plants release oxygen, reduce airborne particulates, regulate the temperature, reduce run-off and stabilise the soil, while providing nesting sites for birds and vital habitat for insects, small mammals and other forms of life. Sites like Camberwell Cemeteries should be celebrated, not razed: as places for the dead to rest peacefully, nature to flourish, and local people to enjoy.

14 July 2018

There are some animals that even zoologists struggle not to ascribe human characteristics to, and one is the stoat. Brimful of mischief and personality, these handsome little rascals are brave, bold and bloodthirsty, and unless you happen to be a gamekeeper an encounter with one will most likely make your day.

Scout was investigating a sandy bank riddled with rabbit burrows. As I called her away, something half-hidden in the summer-brown grass caught my eye, moving in a way I didn't recognise. It wasn't a rabbit, rook, wood pigeon or pheasant, the four most likely options; as for a squirrel, the gait – low and undulating – was similar, but the colour wasn't right.

It was a stoat, and like Scout it was investigating the warren, but unlike her it was narrow enough to go in. A fast, deadly little predator able to dispatch a coney four times its weight with a bite to the back of the neck and drag it great distances, stoats are known for 'dancing' to

mesmerise their prey, and rabbits in particular can become paralysed by their antics, allowing them to approach closely enough to kill.

Quietly, I brought Scout to heel and shaded my eyes, and as I did so it mounted a molehill, stood up on its back legs and stared back at me; and so we regarded one another levelly – as equals, I couldn't help but feel. 'Our eyes locked, and someone threw away the key,' Annie Dillard wrote of the stoat's smaller cousin the weasel in her essay collection *Teaching a Stone to Talk: Expeditions and Encounters*; 'our look was as if two lovers, or deadly enemies, met unexpectedly on an overgrown path where each had been thinking of something else.'

Stoats have an excellent sense of smell, but luckily I was walking into the wind. As I slowly moved closer, admiring its round ears, black button eyes and creamy chest, it seemed just as curious about me. At last, discretion got the better of valour and it popped down into a burrow, and though I waited with Scout for more than ten minutes, it did not reappear.

We've been plagued in recent weeks by common pollen beetles (*Brassicogethes aeneus*). These greenish-black two-millimetre-long flying beetles are a major pest of oilseed rape and other crucifers, reducing yields and even destroying entire crops. They occasionally explode into great numbers, filling the air to the delight of swifts, swallows and house martins, and spreading out over large stretches of land. They're particularly drawn to the colour yellow, and in the village we've all had to stop wearing anything that might attract them when we're out and about.

Pollen beetles have begun developing resistance to common insecticides like pyrethroids, and research is ongoing into seriochemical strategies (for instance pheromones), traps that emit certain wavelengths of light, and other holistic methods of control. This research is vital: we must find ways to support farmers in producing the crops we rely on, while broadening our arsenal to prevent further resistance, and reducing our reliance on the insecticides implicated in the devastating collapse in insect numbers that's taken place on our watch.

Between the parched barley, wheat and maize about ten minutes' walk from my cottage stands a veteran oak estimated to be about seven hundred years old, and recently I climbed it at dusk and sat quietly as the sun sank slowly into the fields. Out of sight, and with my scent carried about fifteen feet above anything at ground level, I was almost undetectable, and I watched as one by one hares came out to feed, painted golden in the last rich rays of light. Over the course of forty minutes or so the birds went to sleep: a distant song thrush quieted, pheasants alarumed and then were still, and the last rooks rowed over in the darkening sky. And then the night shift: just as I was about to climb down, a little owl dropped from the next oak to forage for invertebrates among the young maize.

Nine to 10 p.m. is prime time in the TV schedules, when I'd usually be on the sofa bathed in flickering blue light. It was good to remind myself that while we're at our most domestic the natural world continues beyond our drawn curtains: unpredictable, extraordinary, out of sight.

18 August 2018

Heat for weeks on weeks; no rain at all since early May. In East Anglia the earth was baked, the grass long gone; only the deeper-rooted weeds still showed green here and there: plantain, dandelion, bindweed coiling up from somewhere far underground. In the drought, *Orthoptera* thrived: the meadow in front of my cottage was abuzz with grasshoppers by day, while dark bush-crickets sang in the village gardens through each stifling, clammy night. Flies swarmed indoors, far more than usual; birds, sheltering from the blazing sun, fell daily into my flue and had to be released, panicking, from the empty woodburner.

Out in the cracked and fissured fields the wheat was harvested, and then the barley: the golden acres, dry as tinder, had looked wonderful below the hard blue bowl of the sky, but yields were poor. The ford was dry, the ditches empty. The water level in the river sank low, and then lower. Crop fires saw the cancellation of some local trains.

And then, at last, the weather broke. Warm rain hammered the corn stubble and drenched the parched meadows, releasing heady, fragrant petrichor, washing our sandy soil straight off the fields to block the drains and flooding the lower-lying roads. Weed seeds germinated, and within two days tiny cotyledons carpeted my tired flowerbeds; a few days more and a fresh green aftermath appeared where acres of blond barley had once waved.

At night I lay in bed and listened to the rain pattering on the roof and gurgling in the gutters, picturing the damp, brown fields, the water refilling the ditches and all the grateful frogs and toads – those that have made it through the heatwave – once again able to move about. It can't be easy, being an amphibian in a dry spell, or even a hedgehog, come to that: until a couple of days ago I hadn't seen a living slug, snail or worm since spring. Small wonder: weeks of stifling heat have made life hard for anything that needs to be moist.

As global temperatures warm, summers like this will fast become more frequent. Not all of our precious wildlife will prove able to adapt.

One native creature hardest hit by drought is the mole, which explains why there was one above ground in my garden recently, and many similar reports on social media in recent weeks. The sound of gravel being flung about had made me open the back door, expecting to find a foraging blackbird; instead, what I saw was a velvety black creature with a pink nose and huge paws energetically exploring the damp earth under my garden tap. Parched soil can't support the worms and grubs moles rely on for food and moisture, so long dry spells see millions die. Unwelcome as they are in most gardens, I could not begrudge this one its desperate bid to survive.

I fetched my phone and managed to shoot a quick video, as it was the first mole I'd ever seen alive above ground; though he froze at my approach, Maurice (as I named him) seemed to believe that if his head was hidden by gravel I couldn't see his backside. Sadly, this misapprehension may be what makes moles frequent prey for all the local cats.

The swifts have gone from our skies, and with them each year goes the best of summer: a fulcrum tips now towards autumn that doesn't tip on midsummer night. There are house martins still, and swallows; but the air is empty of the swifts' black sickles, and their joyful screams. Without them the world seems so suddenly, desolately quiet.

22 September 2018

Knowing my interests, a friend has brought me as a gift a lovely little book once owned by her mother. Called *Every Day in the Country*, it was written by one Harrison Weir, best known as a watercolourist, cat fancier and pigeon and poultry expert, and published in 1883. The left-hand pages inform the reader what they may expect to observe in the countryside on each and every day of the year, with space on the right (largely untaken in my copy) for their own notes and records. So on 11 January we learn that 'Earth Worms lie out', while on 3 July 'Chaffinch's song ceases' and on 16 August 'Barley cut'. The entry for 22 September reads: 'Heath in flower. Great Plovers [stone curlews, now amber-listed] assemble. Wood Pigeons flock. Beech Nuts fall.' It is remarkably, and charmingly, precise.

It is also a testament to both change and loss – not only of species (elm trees, great bustards, corncrakes . . .), or even abundance, but also of cultural traditions, common knowledge and an assumption of cyclical regularity in regard to the natural world. Of course Weir doesn't really expect readers to record each instance on the exact day he notes it, but 135 years ago the seasons certainly arrived with more regularity, weather patterns were more predictable (up to a point) and the effects of both climate change and the intensification of agriculture were a long way off. There is something hypnotic about flicking through the pages with their confident invocations of the changeless seasonality of insects, birds, fish and flowers. It is, at an atavistic level, deeply comforting – until one shuts the book.

Today the People's Walk for Wildlife will take place in our capital city, a way for growing numbers of people who realise what is happening to the natural world to come together and be visible. It is not too late to change our relationship with nature for the better. It is not too late to win back what we have lost.

*

Last weekend, according to *Every Day in the Country*, the goatsucker departed, a beautiful but rather uncanny nocturnal bird that breeds on our heaths and moors each summer and is these days known as the nightjar. When they leave our shores it's thought that they follow a 'loop' migratory pattern, wintering in Central Africa but taking different routes during the spring and autumn migrations.

There are several reasons for the nightjar's eeriness, which exceeds by some measure that of other nocturnal birds like owls. Firstly there's their huge black eyes and breathtakingly cryptic plumage that allows them to rest along a branch, or in leaf litter, and completely disappear. Close up, they resemble some kind of reptile, while in flight, hawking for moths, they resemble most closely a bird of prey.

But it's the males' call that's truly haunting: a low, uninterrupted churr that sounds a bit like a distant Moog synthesiser left on repeat. Twice this summer I've heard nightjars at dusk on nearby Dunwich Heath. It never fails to raise the fine hairs on the back of my neck.

Walking home after the village's Harvest Supper, a bright half-moon and a scatter of equinoctial stars overhead, I heard a different kind of nocturnal singer: dark bush-crickets chirping loudly from the verges, hedgerows and front gardens between the village hall and my house. The warm, dry weather this year has worked in their favour, allowing good numbers of their eggs, laid eighteen months ago, to hatch and the nymphs mature.

Dark bush-crickets are now common in southern and central England, though while they were certainly known of in Britain as far back as 1872 I can find no mention of them in *Every Day in the Country*. Global warming has allowed several species of cricket to expand their range north from their Mediterranean strongholds, making them a rare winner to set against our ongoing catalogue of loss.

Overhead, other creatures were calling, although I couldn't hear them: pipistrelle bats flickered silently between me and the stars, their cries too high-pitched now for my adult ears although they were perfectly audible when I was a child. September marks the start of the breeding season and the time, too, when bats must begin laying down fat stores for winter. For while the trees are mostly still green, the year is turning. Autumn, in whatever form it comes now, is here.

27 October 2018

This week I found a dead weasel and put it in my stocking. No, it's not a nursery rhyme, a euphemism or the elaborate set-up for a joke: the mustelid in question was lying at the base of a hedge not far from my cottage, cause of death unknown. I picked it up and took it home to photograph, then buried it in the garden near the dear departed goldfinch I found a little while ago, marking the spot with a stick. I'll dig it up again in a couple of months, by which time the skeleton will only require a little dilute hydrogen peroxide to clean up well.

And the hosiery, you ask? It's a neat trick to keep all the bones together once they begin to disarticulate. It's easy to lose things like teeth and tiny phalanges (foot bones) in the soil. One of the things I'd most hate to mislay is the baculum or penis bone, if present. (I didn't sex my weasel for reasons I won't go into here out of respect for reader sensitivities.) I'm also keen to find out whether the skull shows damage to the nasal sinus characteristic of *Skrjabingylus nasicola*, a parasitic nematode and something you'll definitely regret looking up online. Weasels can be infected in the course of eating shrews, another host, and the parasite could even be the cause of my specimen's death. Some naturalists have speculated as to whether the erratic 'dancing' behaviour sometimes observed in both stoats and weasels could actually be caused by the maddening discomfort of an advanced *Skrjabingylus* infection.

Weasels are our smallest mustelid, fast, fierce, fluid and incredibly charismatic. Death had drawn the lips of my little corpse back, showing off its tiny, pure-white, razor-sharp teeth: a beautiful, pitiless killing machine as perfectly evolved to fill its ecological niche as the worm that sets up home in its nose.

I've been hearing a lot of tawny owls in recent weeks, calling to attract a mate or establish a territory. Autumn is when this year's youngsters disperse and pairs form; those that fail to establish and defend an area big enough to supply them with prey will quickly perish, so the stakes are high.

While at primary school I learned a short section from *Love's Labour's Lost* off by heart, including the lines 'Then nightly sings the staring owl, / Tu-whit; / Tu-who, a merry note'. I remember thinking that it didn't actually sound very merry at all. Later, of course, I discovered that owls don't sing *tu-whit tu-whoo* anyway; that in fact, the sound pattern is formed from a contact call more accurately rendered as *ke-WICK!*, which is answered, by a second owl, with a *whoo-oo-oo*.

While visiting my friend Saskia in Somerset we took her Labrador, Nora, for a seaside walk at Stolford. The track to the beach was loud with squabbling sparrows and starlings sheltering in a dense bramble bank behind which a few houses sheltered, in turn, from the brisk sea wind. The sea wall and salt marsh were busy with meadow pipits ('mipits') and wagtails picking invertebrates from the warm stone and sheep-cropped grass, while on the beach colourful shelducks – one of our largest ducks, almost as big as a goose – worked the sand and shallow water, looking for lunch. There were beadlet anemones glinting like cushion-cut garnets in the rock pools, and here and there the partial hieroglyphs of Rhaetian-era ammonites marked the smooth beach pebbles made of blue lias stone laid down over 200 million years ago.

As we walked with our eyes down, looking for the spiral-shaped ghosts of long-dead marine creatures, the vast grey blocks of Hinkley Point B nuclear power station squatted cryptically in the distance, the dull, unchanging roar of its turbines underlying the mewing calls of the gulls.

1 December 2018

December afternoons do something to my heart. Perhaps it's the early dusk combined with approaching winter: a sense of drawing-in, of lighting the lamps early, and the fire; the way a tiny village like mine huddles together in its landscape, its encircling fields ploughed to brown, its hedgerows bare. In December the windows of our cottages glow yellow from half past three or four o'clock; as the light fails, rooks in skeins and then single stragglers return to their ancient rookery in the trees by the river to caw themselves to sleep. Later, shy roe deer emerge invisibly from the woods and spinneys to pace the footpaths where, by day, we walk our dogs; in the village lanes, the deer's clustered droppings tell us that they pass among our little houses while we sleep.

The moon is at its highest and whitest on December nights, reaching the centre of the sky where there's less of the earth's polluted atmosphere to dull its light. Walking the two kilometres back from the station to my cottage last Friday night, when it was full, the fields looked spectral: utterly bleached of colour, yet clearly illumined: a strikingly unfamiliar visual effect. The moon-shadow of the hedge bordering the lane stretched out across the tarmac, crisp and detailed; beside me, my moon-shadow kept pace with me as I walked. When a cloud moved in, the world was plunged into darkness; I looked up in time to see it stream away and that ice-cold light blaze out again. Approaching the village with no need of my torch, I startled a roosting pheasant; its rusty alarm-clock shrieks set another one off, behind the houses, and then another, further off. By the time I got to my front door, half my neighbours were probably awake.

It's at dusk that I feel most keenly the long history of this village, the course of its four narrow lanes set a millennia or more ago, its Norman church and scatter of humble dwellings many hundreds of years old. It persists, as villages do, protecting and outliving its inhabitants: human-made, but having transcended us to become part of its landscape. At their best, rural villages bear witness to a lasting partnership of people, place and nature, and to me there is something deeply moving – almost sacred – about that.

My neighbour has been mushrooming, and I envy him his knowledge – and his confidence. He sets out with a wicker basket and home-made tool fashioned from a paintbrush with a blade bound into the handle, returning with blewits, ceps or even the sponge-like mass of a *Sparassis*. Like most people I'm far too chary to follow suit, even armed with a field guide; the dreadful fate that befell Nicholas Evans, author of *The Horse Whisperer* (he received a kidney from his daughter after accidentally poisoning himself and three other people) linger too vividly in my mind. 'I've been doing this all my life,' my neighbour reassures me; 'although there are fewer and fewer every year.' Then he breaks into sudden laughter: 'Perhaps I'm the problem!' he says, and disappears indoors to fry his bounty for lunch.

In some places commercial foraging to supply the restaurant trade is reducing fungal biodiversity, and the National Trust and City of London Corporation have had to ban mushroom-picking in certain areas. In the wider countryside, though, it's a great shame that lack of knowledge is causing the loss of vital experiential contact with our natural surroundings.

Now is the season when spindles reveal their glory. For most of the year so unobtrusive as to be almost invisible, in late autumn, as everything else dies back, these extraordinary little trees burst out in a bright, almost tropical display. Their bulbous hot-pink fruits split open in four petal-like sections to reveal a bright-orange aril, fleshy but poisonous to humans. The effect is one of antic blossom in an otherwise bleak scene.

Spindles fared badly in the 1960s and 1970s when they were identified as the winter host of an arable crop pest, leading (in part) to many miles of hedgerows being grubbed up. Now, though, wildlife-friendly farmers appreciate this native species' value to our declining wildlife. Spindle leaves are the food source for many species of moth and butterfly; in spring and summer its nectar and sap support a wide range of insects and they, in turn, attract birds – some of which also eat the fruits later in the year. Not for nothing is the spindle tree known in Germany as *Rotkehlchenbrot*, or 'robin's bread'.

5 January 2019

Passing a field of winter wheat in the strange, dull days between Christmas and New Year, what I'd assumed to be a molehill suddenly resolved itself, like one of those Magic Eye paintings, into a hare, eyes wide and ears flat back. Spellbound, I watched from only a few feet away as it gradually flattened its body, knowing itself observed; after a few moments I moved on, elated, so as not to cause it any more stress. Hares – and leverets particularly – are known for often remaining still as humans approach, relying for survival on their camouflage (and our poor observational skills).

The way other living things flee from us has, I believe, left a deep unconscious scar. We walk into a landscape and it all but empties: birds drop from the leeward side of trees and glide away; small mammals scurry into the undergrowth; deer fade into the woods; rabbits bolt. It is, perhaps, why we keep pets: to have the company of creatures other than ourselves. It may also be why experiences such as swimming with dolphins are so powerfully trans-formative, allowing us briefly to feel accepted into the wild world, rather than cast out.

Despite a nationwide decline of about 80 per cent in the last century, East Anglia is known as a stronghold for brown hares, and in the fields around my village there's a healthy population, largely due to good farming practices. So the news that myxomatosis, a deadly rabbit virus deliberately introduced from South America in the 1950s, may have made the jump to hares is devastating. Researchers at the University of East Anglia are looking into a spate of unex-plained hare deaths from across the UK, with symptoms in some cases identical to those produced by myxomatosis. (Other diseases, such as European brown hare syndrome and coccidiosis, have not yet been ruled out.)

But amid an outpouring of concern online, one strand stood out: 'Why is it dreadful news? They are not a native species' read one tweet from a self-professed naturalist. Brown hares have lived for two thousand years on these islands, are ecologically integrated and feature strongly in our shared heritage of folklore and legend, yet to some they don't belong, and their suffering is of no consequence. What strange times these are, in which ideas of purity and nativism can affect our sympathies – even when it comes to our threatened natural world.

The hedges and verges have died back enough to reveal their secret cargoes of energy drink cans, fast-food packaging, wet wipes, fag packets, juice boxes and knotted poo bags, deposited by dog owners, thrown out of car windows, dropped by kids or blown from overfull bins. Because I'm always on foot I see more of it than I would from a car, so I keep a carrier bag with me and, when I'm passing, fill it up. I've twice borrowed a grabber and litter-picked the lane to the station too, each time filling two black sacks. 'You'll never get it all!' one driver called out cheerfully, as though that rendered any effort pointless; 'You're making me feel bad for not doing the same,' said a dog walker, in tones of distinct admonishment. 'Well, why not start?' I replied with a smile.

It's the bagged poo that irritates me most, as a (responsible) dog owner. Why bag it up only to abandon it – or, worse, hang it on a bush or fence? It makes no sense to me at all.

I miss them, but the silence of the birds is all part of winter's character. This time of year is about conserving energy, rather than the joyous excess that warm weather, abundant food and the breeding instinct bring. But birdsong may still be heard now and again, and seems to carry an extra layer of defiance – from robins' year-round pugnacity to the insistent two-note song of a great tit broadcasting his hopes, on a bright, cold day, for an early spring. Song thrushes sometimes tune up in the grottiest weather; what's far less common is for a blackbird to sing in the winter months. And yet, two weeks ago, I heard one while walking up a farm track in freezing drizzle: a sound utterly evocative of spring and early summer, but rarely heard from August on. It took a while for my brain to resolve the cognitive dissonance produced by the contrast between what I could see and feel around me, and what I could hear. 'If the blackbird sings before Christmas, he will cry before Candlemas' runs one old saying; in which case, expect raw weather before 2 February.

9 February 2019

Running from the heart of my little village to the farm shop is a path locally known as 'the carnser', an old East Anglian word meaning a raised causeway over boggy ground. In late spring and early summer it's intoxicating, a narrow path through tall, lush vegetation with glimpses on one side across a low-lying field to the pretty houses of the village, and on the other into a five-acre meadow belonging to my friends Sue and Richard, and beautifully managed for wildlife. In February it is muddy, with a starker beauty and a clearer sense of having been laboriously built up higher than the surrounding flood plain many centuries ago.

A wooden bridge crosses the River Ore, from the banks of which osiers were once cut for basketwork; we know this from field names recorded on old tithe maps. No market for osiers now, but the river is home to precious otters; they've been caught on camera traps and occasionally leave temporary insignia on the banks in prints and jasmine-smelling spraint.

At last the A-road roars into view, insisting on the modern world, laden with lorries, hell to cross on foot. I have an old photograph showing it when it was nothing more than an unmade lane that crossed the river on a quaint, humpbacked bridge; I can stand on the spot where it was taken and match up one or two surviving timber buildings, but I cannot quite convince my mind that the present road truly developed from that narrow, rustic lane.

Sometimes, walking Scout, I take an invisible, unsignposted route across a nearby field, taking as a sightline two oaks that were probably once part of a hedgerow long grubbed up. In summer, when the crops are high, the farmer mows a line for villagers to follow; now, only my memory of last summer tells me that a path is there. As I slog through mud along the ghost route I think about the carnser, carrying villagers over the stoachy water meadow for centuries; and about the A-road, as brutal and anonymous now as any other, busily erasing its past.

My line across the field passes under another: power cables march across it on tall poles. Glowing amber in the low winter sun, a male kestrel grips a wire with citrine feet and, beak tucked into breeze-ruffled chest, regards the foolish human toiling below. Even when I am directly under him, gazing up, he doesn't budge – and why should he when all the cold blue sky is his, when all he has to do is unclutch his talons, open his wings and wheel away?

I've been seeing kestrels almost daily in recent weeks, and it speaks well of the richness of life in the fields and hedges hereabout. Our most numerous bird of prey, they eat small mammals such as voles, amphibians and reptiles, and invertebrates such as caterpillars, grasshoppers and slugs; they will also sometimes take small birds from cover, rather than in flight as the sparrowhawk will.

When hunting, kestrels can hang almost motionless in the air for long periods, hence their lovely country name of windhover. In the sixteenth century, though, they were known as windfucker or fuckwind, the vulgar word probably then meaning 'to beat or strike'.

At last, the shy snowdrops have arrived to light up the woods and verges like tiny, candle-carrying nuns. They seem to me both brave and supplicatory; their white coifs modest, their eyes cast down. Amid the mud and the cold, wet leaf litter they remain pure and inviolate: tiny, delicate harbingers of spring.

Yet they are tough as old boots, with hardened leaf-tips that can break up and out through frozen soil, and anti-freeze as proof against the worst of the weather, keeping them flowering undaunted through frost and snow. Should they briefly slump, they'll always recover to hold their heads up once again.

I've never seen anywhere with as many snowdrops as this village. There are crowds of them in the copses, massed choirs in the churchyard, pious vistas glimpsed through sparse winter hedges and congregations lining the margins of the carnser. 'Spring will come,' they whisper to me quietly as dull winter drags on and on. 'Have faith.'

16 March 2019

The past is a foreign country; the wildlife is much more abundant there. Visiting my father, who still lives in the Surrey village where I grew up, I was struck by how busy the roads were, how tidy and managed it seemed compared to the rambling, slightly ramshackle place I remember – and how little space was left for the natural world. Everything that wasn't built on was strimmed and pruned, every green glimpse a monoculture paddock or tightly manicured golf course, the tangled woods I once played in tidied up and fenced off for paintball. It looked pretty and prosperous – but as money poured in to create this stockbroker-belt simulacrum of an English arcadia, the wildlife was quietly forced out.

In the last thirty years, 11.5 per cent of Surrey's plants, birds, invertebrates, fish, reptiles, amphibians and mammals have become locally extinct – a far higher figure than the national rate of 2 per cent. A further 4.4 per cent are threatened with extinction, and many more are in serious decline. There's no agribusiness or heavy industry to take the blame; instead, the numbers tell part of the story: it may look bucolic from the 8.02 to Waterloo, but Surrey ranks in the top 25 per cent of England's most densely populated counties, with most above it metropolitan, such as Bristol, Greater London, Greater Manchester and Merseyside.

This degradation is happening everywhere, to varying extents – but it hits hard to see it on your own patch. The garden I played in as a child was home to hedgehogs, toads and lizards; it supported a huge range of birds (including now-scarce lesser spotted woodpeckers) and danced with moths and butterflies. There was too much sometimes: we'd scoop binloads of spawn from the choked pond each March and take it to Bolder Mere near Wisley, where we'd pour the gelatinous armfuls in. But now there are no hedgehogs, toads or lizards in Dad's garden, the range of birds on his feeder is much narrower, and in spring only a few stray frogs breed in his pond – unsurprising, as a full half of the county's amphibians are in decline.

Surrey may be full to bursting, but it's not lacking in back gardens, and that's where a sea change must now occur. Nature needs untidiness in order to flourish; it must be allowed to be self-willed, not made to look like something from a glossy magazine.

One way to help stabilise insect and amphibian numbers across the UK is to create thousands more ponds. The Wildlife Trusts and the Royal Horticultural Society have come together for the Wild About Gardens campaign, which this year aims to get more of us to either dig a pond of any size in our gardens or create a mini water feature

from an upcycled, planted-up, rainwater-filled sink or washing-up bowl.

Passing through my old home town of Guildford I was shocked to see several mature trees covered with huge nets, and quickly snapped a picture. There's been a recent rash of developers trying to prevent birds nesting in this way, as once they do they cannot legally be disturbed; it's a deeply cynical ploy, and one that does not sit well at all with the general public, as I found. I sent a tweet, which garnered thousands of retweets and replies and led to the local council stepping in and having the nets removed by the developer – who, it emerged, had not even secured planning permission for the site.

Of course, if the development goes ahead there will be ecological surveys and 'biodiversity offsetting' should be put in place – which can mean little more than planting non-native saplings in place of mature native trees. But some site-faithful birds such as sparrows (which are in decline) rarely move more than a kilometre from the place of their birth; the loss of suitable breeding habitat for a couple of seasons can wipe out a small colony. This, I realised, is how we lose our wildlife: bit by bit by bit.

Yet perhaps the tide of public opinion is turning against this kind of rapaciousness. Some environmental losses may be hard to picture, but when faced with the stark image of a tree in which birds cannot nest, we know in our bones that it's wrong.

20 April 2019

These April mornings break slow with bright birdsong. First, robins tune up in dark village gardens, hesitant, apologetic; the sky's still pitch, with just the first suggestions of a glow behind the easternmost cottages, beyond fields sown to young wheat and bounded by the grey A-road. Not much is moving on it yet: the odd taxi, some farm traffic, a few early risers. Rabbits nibble its dim verges, lit only occasionally by passing headlights; a crow picks at the smashed jigsaw of a pheasant and a barn owl drifts to its roost over a roadside paddock, disappearing, unremarked, out of sight.

In the village, the silvery robins have been joined by the flutier, jollier carolling of blackbirds and the scratchy scribbles of dunnocks' hedge-top songs. As we villagers doze on, or roll over in bed crossly, gangs of sparrows set about the morning's gossip, wrens shrill, and great tits begin turning all their squeaky wheels. From chimneypot and aerial the complacent coos of collared doves drop like slow, cool water into the busy current of song.

As the sky lightens, the still-sleeping village comes chorusing to life. Greenfinches are calling now, and chaffinches and blue tits; the rooks are awake, cawing gutturally from nests in the early-leafed horse chestnut and the precious, surviving elm behind my neighbours' house. So too are the local cockerels, who yell indignantly to one another: one from a garden near the church, one further away, across a field.

And out in those fields the dawn chorus continues, the sad, gappy hedges still host to yellowhammers' insistent chirruping, the copses loud with the lovely repetitions of song thrushes, the uninflected *dink-dink-dink* of chiff-chaffs not long in from Africa and the irresolute remarks of the blackcap, its timbre somewhere between the robin's and the blackbird's. It's hard to believe that in a month there'll be more summer migrants and even greater volume; harder still to comprehend that the breathtaking dawn chorus we're still lucky enough to be able to hear each spring is a shadow of what it once was, even one generation ago.

The old earth turns, rolling night's shadow back. The village cockerels are abashed into silence, the last fussing pheasant gathers its few wits and quietens, and a new day breaks. As the first smartphone alarm sounds its harsh little ditty, over the wheat a lark invisibly, endlessly sings.

Noon, and the April sun illuminates the verges with their embroidery of spring flowers. Near our little village hall a long bank has been colonised by the ghostly bells of drooping star of Bethlehem; among it, celandines and dark, elfin dog violets, scentless but pretty, glimmer here and there. White dead-nettle and the bright brass buttons of dandelions, beloved of bees, line the lanes, and the paddock where rescue ponies grazed last year is now a purple haze of *Glechoma hederacea*, a fragrant perennial once used to flavour beer, whose country names include alehoof, tunhoof, gill-over-the-ground, ground-ivy, creeping charlie, catsfoot, run-away-robin and field balm.

By late afternoon the light is low and golden, picking out the texture of our old flint walls and Suffolk bricks. On the water meadow and in the molehill-stippled field by the church the rabbits are out feeding: dun shapes lit gold by the lowering sun. The village cats, I'm told, are making short work of the warrens' kits; there are stoats and weasels too here, and I'm sure they're doing the same.

My back-garden blackbird concludes his evening recital, performed amid the blush-pink blossom of an apple tree planted a quarter of a century ago. The last song thrushes still shout from the tangled spinneys; it won't be long now, I hope, until the village's two male nightingales return to sing in our night-time woods in hopes of attracting a mate. Last year one paired but the other, who chose a spot near the main road, didn't, his song perhaps drowned out by passing cars. With nightingale numbers in such steep decline, we can ill afford to lose even a single set of chicks.

On the acres of rape past the church and across the stream the bird scarer goes off for the final time. A timed, gas-powered cannon that emits deafening bangs, it keeps pigeons (and dog walkers) away from the crop in daylight hours. As the last report fades, peace returns to the little cluster of houses with yellow-lit windows. Then a barn owl floats slow above the lane to the next village, a silent ghost setting out into the fading light.

25 May 2019

A little delayed by a cold north wind, like many of our summer migrants, thirty thousand or so cuckoos have now arrived back in Britain. One has set up shop in my village, his evocative two-note song echoing lazily across the water meadow all morning, issuing from a copse at sunset and encouraging us villagers on our regular litter-picking afternoon.

A staple of *The Times*'s letters page for many decades, for as little as seven weeks cuckoos will be heard in those parts of our countryside where enough habitat survives to support them, in terms of both food sources (large, hairy moth caterpillars) and the species in whose nests they lay their eggs. A declining Red List bird, research has shown that the UK's cuckoos follow two return routes to the Congo Basin after breeding, one of which – via Spain and Morocco – exposes them to greater mortality risk at their stopover sites. Add fast-declining moth numbers to the picture and the real surprise is that we have any left at all.

Given the widespread condemnation of nest predators such as magpies – which leads some bird lovers to trap and kill them – it's surprising how few harbour similar feelings towards the cuckoo, an obligate brood parasite whose offspring, once hatched in a foster parents' nest, set about heaving rival chicks and eggs out so that the hapless parents are not distracted from the mammoth task of rearing such a massive (and hungry) dependant. The fact that this natural but grisly process happens largely unseen, in open countryside, instead of in the gardens and nest boxes we consider our personal protectorates, may have a great deal to do with it.

Cuckoos' recent rarity also makes us more forgiving of their habits, and when they were more numerous human attitudes were more censorious. Chaucer decried them as 'unkynde' and a 'mortherere' (murderer), and Shakespeare believed that fledgling cuckoos ate their foster parents. Even the scientifically minded Gilbert White called their behaviour 'a monstrous outrage'. Perhaps in these socially progressive times we have a greater tolerance for atypical family structures, but more likely it's a case of 'out of sight, out of mind'.

One of my favourite things to do on warm spring evenings is climb the huge veteran oak not far from my cottage and watch the sun go down over the fields. I've even been known to take a bottle of wine.

I've watched all sorts of creatures from my vantage point: hares boxing only a few yards away, little owls dropping from a neighbouring tree to eat beetles among the young maize, great spotted woodpeckers drilling the branches above me, roe deer stepping cautiously out of the copses, and of course the usual farmland denizens: rooks, pheasants and rabbits.

There are baby rabbits everywhere right now, and sitting in my oak I watched an alert doe shepherd four kits out from the warren by the field path to feed. In *Watership Down*, Richard Adams called the dawn and dusk feeding periods 'silflay'; they're timed to maximise the chances of dew being on the ground, as rabbits, a vulnerable prey species, avoid congregating to drink from puddles or streams. The evening sun picks them out as they play, gold-edged and painterly: humble but quite lovely in the low, warm light.

While on the village litter-pick I had ample time to consider what's become a ubiquitous but barely regarded blight on the environment. I don't mean rubbish (though that is a serious issue), but over-tidiness: road verges mown in full bloom when there's no visibility issue, valuable dead wood cleared away, hedges topped from habit twice yearly, making them useless as wildlife habitats or corridors, and urban pavements, paths and the bases of park trees sprayed with glyphosate to prevent any unsanctioned eruption of life.

As in Surrey, this mania for tidiness is eradicating wildflowers, butterflies, insect- and seed-eating birds, hedgehogs and a whole host of other creatures we profess to love. So why are we letting it happen? I think it's crept up on us slowly, so that we simply can't see the harm we're doing. Just as we believe the number of insects around us is normal, rather than terrifyingly depleted, it looks right to us now for verges to be razed rather than riotous, and for farmland hedges to look ugly and smashed. We've also been slow to wake up to how crucial these vestiges of habitat have become for wildlife, as pressures on the wider countryside have invisibly mounted up. To turn things around requires a paradigm shift: can we tolerate an untidier, bushier, scrubbier environment to help bring nature back?

29 June 2019

I returned from a week's walking holiday in the Austrian Tyrol to find that a growth spurt fed by sunshine and showers had turned my front garden into a firework box of lupins, and the few feet of lawn at the back into a mini wildflower meadow. I was thrilled by how full of life it all was, from the broad-bordered bee hawkmoth my neighbour emailed me about while I was halfway up an Alp to the froghopper nymphs wrapped in gobs of cuckoo-spit in the long grass and even the aphids encrusting the older lupin stems – fantastic news for my local sparrows, as they rely on aphids to feed their young. Watching the adult birds cling to the tall stems to pick them off, ferrying beakful after beakful to their importunate young, made me feel proud to supply food for a new generation of these cheerful but declining birds.

Kate Bradbury's wildlife gardening segments on *Springwatch* – now collected together on BBC iPlayer as *Wild in the Garden* – have given me a new way to look at my garden, one in which many of the things I'd grown up thinking of as 'pests', a nuisance or unsightly, are vital elements in a complex web of life. To see Kate plant rose varieties specifically because their soft foliage will be good for leafcutter bees gave me a glimpse of the pleasure that might come from a different kind of custodianship, one whose measure isn't success with exotic cultivars or perfect floral borders, but about making a space that helps feed and house the cast of creatures we all grew up with, many of which are now slipping away.

I thought about insects a lot when I was on holiday, and how fundamental they are to the survival of birds, bats, small rodents and all sorts of other creatures further up the food chain. I walked in ancient, unimproved Alpine meadows, still cut by hand and untreated with biocides, that contained a dizzyingly diverse mix of grasses and wildflowers: bladder campion, red and white clover, pignuts, chamomile, toadflax, dandelions, vetches, arnica, speedwell, buttercups, and, in the higher pastures, pasque flowers, velvetbells, wild crocuses, mountain primroses and gentians so staggeringly blue they hurt the eyes. Because of this diversity, there were insects everywhere, too many to count or even for me to recognise: day-flying moths, bees of various kinds, spiders, flying beetles, fat field crickets, flies, forest ants, shield bugs, grasshoppers, and on one steep path to a summer farm where the bell-clonking cattle had just been led to graze, perhaps a hundred tiny blue butterflies that billowed up from a muddy patch of ground and enveloped me like a cloud.

Austria's agri-environment programme, ÖPUL, subsidises farmers to improve and protect biodiversity, improve water management and purity, prevent erosion, retain traditional rural knowledge, reduce greenhouse gas emissions and boost carbon sequestration. Added to that, the valley I stayed in was an organic, silage-free zone where cows graze the high pastures in summer and in winter are fed almost entirely on naturally dried hay. 'Haymilk' has been shown to be much lower in *Clostridia* bacteria than milk from silage-fed animals – *Clostridia* is anaerobic and can thrive in plastic-wrapped bales of fermented grass – which is vital, as the fragrant, long-ripened, preservative-free *Heumilchkäse* (haymilk cheese), produced in the Alps for centuries, is made with raw milk.

One of the most common flowers in the Austrian meadows was yellow-rattle, whose old country names include pots and pans, hen pennies, shacklecaps, tiddibottles and gowk's shilling in Scotland (*gowk* meaning 'cuckoo'). A semi-parasitic annual sometimes referred to as 'the meadow-maker', it takes some of its nutrients from vigorous species like grass and clover, preventing them from overgrowing and outcompeting other plants. When it dies off in autumn it leaves useful gaps for other species to colonise, and it is also the food plant for the larvae of two rare moths. In times gone by it was sometimes regarded as a nuisance, as too much of it in a field could reduce hay yields; nowadays, as we try to restore and protect biodiversity, we have a better understanding of the important job it does.

Like glow-worms, corncrakes and many other endangered species, plants such as yellow-rattle, cowslips and orchids evolved to take advantage of traditional haymaking techniques similar to those still practised in the Tyrol today. Austria has found a way to value its flower-rich grassland, benefitting biodiversity, farmers, international tourism – and cheese lovers. Given that only 3 per cent of Britain's wildflower meadows survive, surely the time has come for us to do the same.

27 July 2019

My doorstep is covered in animal faeces, and I couldn't be happier about it. For ten days or so now I've opened the front door to find the mat liberally sprinkled with tiny black droppings, with more scattered in a close semicircle around. Having spotted one caught in a spider's web and another on the wood of the door itself, I realised they must have been falling from somewhere above. It turns out I have a bat roost – or perhaps even a maternity colony! – in a crevice over my front door.

I knew there were lots of bats in the village; I'd sat in my back garden a few nights before, with a friend and a bottle of red, and watched them swooping and flickering not far over our heads. All bats, as well as their breeding sites, are protected, and a healthy population is proof of decent insect numbers and good botanical diversity. Certainly, there are plenty of midges and night-flying moths here, as well as cockchafers – large, gimcrack contraptions also known as maybugs – for larger bat species like noctules or serotines to eat.

Serotines and noctules rarely make their home in buildings. My bats are most likely to be pipistrelles, a tiny rufous bat, small enough to fit in a matchbox, that does a great job of keeping things like mosquitoes down. (One pipistrelle can eat up to three thousand insects per night.)

Bat numbers have fallen fast over the last hundred years, in part due to the ongoing crash in invertebrate abundance, but also because modern buildings rarely provide anywhere for them to live, while insecticides and timber treatments often used on older buildings are also highly toxic to them. Putting up bat boxes can really help; go to www.bats.org.uk for advice.

Having spotted mine emerging one evening, I have a rough idea of size, but I'll need to borrow a detector if I want a really firm ID. Bats are best distinguished by the pitch of their calls; in fact, it was only established in 1999 that there are two entirely separate species of pipistrelle, one echolocating at 45 kHz and the other, the 'soprano pipistrelle', at 55 kHz.

*

Bats aren't the only creatures out at night in the village. Last week I was invited to dinner in Sue and Richard's meadow, which lies between the carnser and the ford. Once it had grown dark we sat around a little shepherd's lantern listening to the persistent begging call of a juvenile tawny owl. On and on it issued from the dark trees, tirelessly, endlessly; the parents must both have gone out hunting, leaving the famished youngster to wonder if it would ever eat again. It must have been hard for the adults to concentrate on the tiny movements of voles and mice, what with all that racket going on.

There are young birds everywhere right now, still just about distinguishable from the adults by their juvenile plumage and – with the exception of those aerial natives the swifts, swallows and house martins – their terrible flying skills. Young male blackbirds are slowly turning blacker; speckled baby robins, still awaiting their orange breast feathers, perch wobblily on my flowerpots, while juvenile blue tits the colour of stonewashed denim whirr awkwardly around in my apple tree. Soon they will grow a proper set of adult feathers and master their wing muscles; for now, I'm enjoying having the clumsy kids around.

It's been a great year for poppies here in Suffolk, their blood-red blooms lining country lanes and dotting the village verges. I walked through one field of chest-high podded rape, the narrow path lined with poppies where the sun had not been shaded out. At the field's far corner a swathe of the crop had been eaten to the ground by roe deer earlier in the year, and here the earth's seedbank had exploded into scarlet: I emerged to find myself walking amid a red, rippling sea of them, laughing out loud with surprise.

Each poppy plant produces an average of seventeen thousand seeds, of which some can lie dormant for up to forty years. This has allowed them to survive the decades in which intensively farmed arable fields were sprayed with powerful herbicides, and they have staged a modest comeback on road verges and field margins since the introduction in the late 1980s of set-aside – an EEC scheme under which a percentage of arable land was taken out of intensive production – and since then, the partial adoption of more wildlife-friendly farming practices.

Their brief season is all but over now. Only one or two still dot the hedge-bottoms, while here and there blow those whose blush has faded in the sun to a pale, papery shade: ghost poppies, haunting the tired August fields.

7 September 2019

It was the sound that reached me first, although I didn't immediately register what it was. I was taking Scout for her third walk of the day (like me, she can't bear to be inside in fine weather), and as we left the village behind a series of high, overlapping whistles blew towards me on the breeze. When we reached a gap in the hedge bordering the lane I peered through and saw them: a dozen lapwings wheeling and dancing over a recently ploughed field.

August marks the end of the breeding season, when our remaining lapwings leave the uplands and begin to flock on pasture, farmland and the shores of estuaries. They'll also be joined by some birds from the Continent who will overwinter with them here.

Also known as green plovers, and peewits, for their signature call, these beautiful waders have a jaunty crest, broad, spade-shaped wings and appear black and white in flight, though their backs are actually a rich, iridescent green. When I was a child, huge flocks were common; I remember seeing them flashing and turning above us, black and white, as we drove across the Somerset Levels on the way back from Devon at the end of our summer holidays.

But like so much of the wildlife we took for granted as children, lapwings have suffered steep declines – down by 80 per cent in England and Wales since 1960 – and are now on the Red List, making a group of twelve birds noteworthy in a way it really shouldn't be. Yet the flocks I remember from my childhood were a shadow of the abundance there once would have been. It is hard for us, with our short lifetimes, to fully experience the losses taking place around us; declines can also seem normal, or somehow inevitable. Certainly, I grew up with the sense that there being less of everything than 'once upon a time' was just the way it was.

Changes in agricultural practices, including the loss of rough grazing, more cultivation of marginal land, a switch to autumn-sown crops and increased use of pesticides, are driving many farmland birds from our fields and skies: curlews and turtle doves, corn buntings, tree sparrows and yellowhammers among them. But this trend is rarely the fault of individual farmers. It is about the economic systems we all participate in, and our collective silence when it comes to asking (and paying) for change.

On a footpath near the village ford lay a dead grass snake perhaps half a metre long. Its back was olive-green, its polished underside beautifully marked in a repeating pattern of yellow and black. Grass snakes sometimes play dead when frightened, opening their mouths, tipping their heads back and remaining still; sadly, though, that wasn't the case this time.

Female grass snakes can grow up to 150 centimetres in length, males to about a metre, and some individuals have been known to live for a quarter of a century. The UK's only egg-laying snake, they eat amphibians almost exclusively; some may even take small fish. While still relatively widespread, locally many populations are declining, falling numbers of frogs, toads and newts – lost through a recent upsurge in waterborne disease and habitat degradation from human activity – being partly to blame.

Yet lack of prey isn't the only threat these shy reptiles face. This one bore tiny, characteristic puncture wounds to its head from an attack by an introduced, widespread, highly predatory species: the domestic cat.

Round my way, harvest has proved a more drawn-out affair than last year, when the summer-long drought ended with stubble fires and the hasty bringing-in of low yields. This year's harvest felt more leisurely and was interrupted by rain, so that the final wheatfield met the combines nearly four weeks after the first.

I walked with Scout across fields to a pub in the next village one warm, still evening at the very end of August. Most were stubble, some newly ploughed; in the distance, square straw bales dotted a buff flank of land like an illustration from a post-war Ladybird book. The air was busy with dragonflies, and swallows hawked low over the soil.

On the way home the light was fading, and from the massy hedgerows came a cool, green smell, as though all the leaves were at last breathing out. I heard the distant roar of machinery, and as I drew close to the village I saw the huge red combine's lights dazzling bright in the dim fields. That night I drifted to sleep listening to the sound of the big machines working not far from my cottage, fading and approaching, fading and approaching, safely gathering in the last of the wheat.

12 *October 2019*

Dartmoor in October can be breathtaking, the high ground brindled with rusting bracken, the woods gold and copper, while clear equinoctial skies reveal views that race away, fold after fold, to the sea. Or it can be grey, windswept and soggy, all distance lost to sheeting rain or low cloud that closes in like wet wool. I rolled the dice; I got the latter. Having written a book about the joys of walking in wet weather, I have lost my right to complain.

Not so the group of damp schoolchildren trailing after their teacher past the deserted medieval village on the slopes of Hound Tor, several of whom seemed less than stoic about the drizzle they were required to traipse through. 'Now, you might think they had an idyllic life here, surrounded by nature,' said the teacher, gesturing at the huddled ruins and misjudging her audience entirely; 'but it was probably actually pretty bleak and tough.'

The children needed no convincing. I wished I could have told them that it was walks like this, on family holidays to Devon, that gave me a resilience I might otherwise lack – as well as a connection to wild places that has proved utterly vital to me in adulthood. But why on earth should they listen? I certainly wouldn't have at that age. 'Rise above it!' my father would tell the six of us kids when we complained about the weather, or feeling tired or cold. We may not have been able to back then, but thanks in part to his example, I mostly can nowadays.

I trudged on, listening to the rain pattering on the hood of my coat. Down in the cleave where the Becka Brook rushed in spate, the rain fell differently. Much was caught by the trees' canopy, which sent it on its way in large, occasional drops instead of the fine, drenching mist of the open moor. Like many of the fragments of ancient woodland on Dartmoor it was a rainforest in miniature, trunks, branches and boulders baized with bright-green moss, the gnarled trees dressed with ferns, epiphytes and elaborate dripping lichen. Everything held moisture; even the peat between the granite clitter oozed and sucked. When at last, half an hour later, a weak sun tentatively came out, I looked back from Black Hill and saw steam rising from the little wood below me, fleeting as breath.

The bird that best embodies Dartmoor for me is the stonechat, its telltale call – exactly like two pebbles being struck together – so recognisable that I was able to identify it on family holidays from quite a young age, sealing its place in my affections. It's a handsome insectivore the size of a robin, the male with a glossy black head, white neck patch and rufous chest, the female better camouflaged but neat and trim nonetheless. They're not hard to find on Devon's uplands; in fact, it's a rare walk on Dartmoor that doesn't feature one perching atop a gorse bush, flicking its wings and bobbing up and down while clinking in alarm at your approach.

'Lonely on fell as chat, / By pot-holed becks / A bird stone-haunting, an unquiet bird', wrote W. H. Auden in 'The Wanderer', far from the first to find their call uncanny. It was once believed that stonechats were able to converse with the devil. They even carried a drop of his blood, marking their chests, and the story went that Old Nick himself would break the spine of anyone who harmed these lovely little birds, or their eggs.

It's common to find the bodies of small rodents around farm buildings; mice can proliferate in barns and stables, while shrews exude an unpleasant taste and are often discarded by cats. But what on first glance I'd assumed to be a wet, dead common shrew near my holiday cottage proved, on closer inspection, to be a harvest mouse (*Micromys minutus*), the first I've ever seen in the wild. A neat row of puncture marks along its spine told the story: it had been gripped some hours before by the talons of a raptor – probably an owl – swallowed whole and then, a little while later, regurgitated.

It wasn't the circumstances in which I'd have liked to first meet one, but I'm still glad to have had the opportunity to take in how tiny they are, how obviously prehensile their tail and how gingery-gold their fur – what of it had survived the raptor's stomach acids, anyway. It's good, too, to know that these lovely little creatures are here at all: numbers are hard to come by, but they're known to be declining, part of the sixth mass extinction that all around us quietly gathers pace.

16 November 2019

I have come to a place of extraordinary silence. Having lived in rural Suffolk for the last two years I thought I knew quiet, but now I've bought my first house, a cottage four miles north in a village significantly further from any main roads – and the difference is astonishing. I didn't consciously notice any traffic noise at my old place, but it must have been there because now, if I wake at night, the silence feels as though it's actively pressing on my ears. Lying in pitch-blackness (we have no street lights), utterly deprived of sensory input, is strangely disquieting. Yet the constant hum of background noise is a very recent development. For most of our history, total silence – and total darkness – would have been nothing unusual at all.

This new quietness has made me more aware of sound, from the mysterious creature that processes across my roof each night to the rain gurgling relentlessly in the gutters and the noise the wind makes as it rushes through the last of the ash leaves, tattered and yellowing. The writer John Lewis-Stempel can tell which part of his wood he's walking through at night by the differing sounds of the leaves overhead; here in my silent village I'm beginning to understand how that might be. The particular whisper of their pinnate leaves, and their flickering, watery shade-pattern, are among the less remarked-upon losses that will attend the possible disappearance of ash trees from our countryside as *Chalara* dieback takes hold.

Sound is such a vital part of our relationship with nature, and yet – apart from birdsong – it's so easily overlooked. Walking with me on Dartmoor last month, my sister Joelle pointed out the hollow thud boots make on fine turf set over dry peat; similarly, there's a clashing sound that comes from walking on wet granite gravel that feels entirely particular to the moor. I wouldn't have said that I could actively hear Scout's footfalls, yet I'm instantly alerted to the fact that she's seen a squirrel or a cat by the sudden silence of her steps.

You can look away from something you're not interested in, but you can't 'listen away' – noises are taken in and processed regardless. We have an auditory relationship with the natural world that persists despite our modern lack of attention to it. Tuning in to sound is a deeply atavistic pleasure.

Once more, the spindles are revealing themselves. Stumbling on one deep in a drab winter wood is enough to bring one up short, the combination of fuchsia and flame so exotic as to seem decidedly un-British – though in fact the spindle is a native tree.

The wood of *Euonymus europaeus* is hard, close-grained and grows straight, making it ideal for winding thread without breaking or catching; it also creates charcoal so smooth as to be prized by artists. Its fruit, bark and leaves were once used to treat lice and nits, and as a purgative.

Despite its long history here, the sixteenth-century herbalist William Turner could find no local names for it, but noted that 'the Duche men call it in Netherlande, "spilboome", that is, spindel-tree, because they use to make spindels of it in that country, and me thynke it may be as well named in English seying we have no other name'.

Dusk is my favourite time to go out walking. As the light fades, the night shift clocks on: rabbits come out to feed, owls call from the copses and spinneys, and foxes, deer, hedgehogs and badgers can sometimes be seen. In summer bats begin hunting as darkness falls, and in spring there is the evening chorus to serenade you, almost as joyful and riotous as at dawn. As the human world quietens down, it can feel as though the natural world wakes up.

But there's another reason I love to be out of doors at day's end. Here in Suffolk traces of the past are everywhere, from horse ponds glinting like mercury among the stubble fields to labourers' cottages like mine with woodsmoke curling from brick chimneys hundreds of years old. In the half-light of dusk, the old lanes empty of traffic, it's possible to leave behind the present day with its frightening uncertainties and enter a world in which heavy horses worked the land, the seasons turned with comforting regularity and climate change was unheard of. Political and social nostalgia may be dangerous, but ecologically it's unavoidable. At dusk – if only briefly – one can imagine that the world is still unharmed.

21 *December* 2019

When house-hunting we all have our priorities: a kitchen big enough to entertain in, maybe, or a highly rated local school. Mine – more important even than a decent garden – was to live within a good network of paths.

Unless I'm ill I walk every day, whether or not Scout is staying with me. Getting out and seeing what the natural world is up to is an essential part of my life, and I don't want to have to get into the car to do it; I just want to sling a coat on, lace up my boots and go. So before buying my Suffolk cottage I studied the local Ordnance Survey maps, looking for the rights of way marked in green, and then I came and walked here, trying to sense what it might be like to tramp them day in, day out, as the seasons changed.

There are enough paths around my new village that I can vary my direction according to the weather and my mood, taking a different route every day of the week if I like. Some are clearly very ancient, linking one part of the village to another, or the village with the distant spire of a neighbouring church; some follow routes once taken by carts and farm wagons, while others seem little more than 'desire paths' made by modern dog walkers out for the obligatory forty-five-minute stroll.

And it's not just we humans that use them; many are trodden by animals too, as the sticky, 'loving', print-preserving mud of the eastern Suffolk claylands attests.

When I first got Scout it surprised me that she would always find and follow a path, however faint it seemed or far ahead she got; what continues to fascinate me now is the fact that wild creatures, from deer to foxes, will take the same line across an open field that humans do.

It happens overhead too; birds have been shown to use roads, canals and roundabouts as waymarkers, following them even when there's a quicker route as the crow (or pigeon, or swallow) flies. Badgers frequently co-opt paths and lanes as the borders of their territories, marking the line of them with a row of latrines.

And it works the other way. More than once, on Dartmoor, I've been forced to follow a sheep track, knowing that however aimlessly it meandered it would at least keep me out of dangerous mires. Who knows how many of the village paths I tread today began as deer tracks or even wolf routes, linking one patch of cover with the next.

Here and there in the bleak winter hedgerows coil garlands of glossy red berries set on twisted, leafless stems. These are not holly but the fruits of bittersweet (*Solanum dulcamara*), a climber also known as woody nightshade. As its name suggests, it thrives in partial shade – in fact, strong sunshine inhibits its growth – and thus it carves out a niche for itself where it doesn't have to compete with vigorous, sun-loving climbers like traveller's joy.

Although its bitter berries can be harmful if eaten in great quantity, woody nightshade should not be confused with deadly nightshade, an unrelated (and much more poisonous) plant. The berries' taste and ill effects are evolutionary ruses to save them from being eaten by anything except birds (for the most part thrushes, blackbirds and fieldfares), which, cleverly, aren't affected. The seeds pass intact through their digestive tracts to be deposited along a different section of hedgeline, ready for a new bittersweet seedling to uncoil.

Once a week or so I set out with a fold-up shopping bag stuffed in my coat pocket to gather kindling, feeling a bit like a medieval peasant from days of yore. Whatever I scavenge I lay out to dry by the woodburner, ready to get the fire going in a few nights' time.

By far my favourite firelighters are pine cones, and I've discovered a small Norway spruce plantation not far away. Huge and mature now, perhaps they were once meant for Christmas trees but somehow missed their chance. Still, they have another midwinter use, for they helpfully drop a great many long, dense cones outside the boundary fence – too many even for the local grey squirrels to eat.

It's not only cheaper but far more fun to lay a fire with foraged kindling, rather than kerosene cubes and shop-bought pine batons. Once properly dry, the spruce cones catch quickly, popping and crackling and giving off a wintry scent far better than any Christmas candle. My winter fires connect me to my local landscape, and to the people who came before me. There is something sacred-seeming about that.

25 January 2020

Winter sun slants low over Suffolk's stubble fields, cold but golden, and casting long shadows. It gilds the brown back of the kestrel as she hovers over a hedgerow, looking for the ultraviolet trails left by the urine of voles passing along their habitual runs. It backlights the tall ears of a hare racing for the wood margin, making them glow pink, and gleams in dustily at the end window of the old barn where, on a beam beside its numbered box, the white owl roosts.

In January the sun never climbs very high, and its position – only around eighteen degrees above the horizon today – means that to reach us it must pass through more of the earth's atmosphere than it does when overhead, scattering the blue end of the spectrum and making the colour temperature of the light very warm. Photographers love to take pictures during the 'golden hour' just after dawn and just before dusk for this very reason: not only is the warm light beautiful, but the long shadows it casts help pick out landscape features like furrows and hedges, creating extraordinary detail and depth. On clear midwinter days with no cloud it is as though the golden hour lasts all day.

Cold, though. The light may be gold, but Suffolk's rich brown ploughland is silvered with a hard frost. No wonder: walking to the pub across the fields the skies were so clear I saw the Milky Way arcing dizzyingly overhead, traversed by four red-winking planes following the same flight path, and punctuated by a brief shooting star. Temperatures plummeted that night, and when I awoke even the tattiest fallen leaves and humblest of field weeds were etched with sparkling silver, as though they were the most precious of jewels. January's low, golden sun fell on them, creating crisp shadows, but could not melt the midnight frost away.

Suffolk in winter may be beautiful, but it's not always peaceful. The woods and fields around my house echo with the sound of gunfire, accompanied by the deeper, percussive booms of gas-powered bird scarers. The pheasant-shooting season ends soon, but the bird scarers will stay in place through spring – one of them aimed squarely at the back of my cottage. Pity poor Scout, impervious to city traffic, crowds and sirens, but so fearful now that on a walk she bolts for home at the first bang, and won't even venture into the back garden for a wee at this time of year.

At night the wood pigeons leave the fields and roost in the village's conifers and other evergreens. Returning from the pub with my torch, I startled several, sending them exploding out of the foliage with much clapping of wings and the characteristic whistling noise their feathers make in flight. They're perfectly capable of dropping silently out of a tree on the far side of an approaching human; this loud take-off is a non-vocal avian alarm call, designed to communicate danger to others. We now know that a specially modified outer wing feather creates the piping sound.

Near the church, winter aconites are coming into bloom. These bright-yellow relatives of the buttercup are unrelated to the true aconites, though their leaves do bear a resemblance; instead, they behave rather like snowdrops, flowering early amid the leaf litter, taking advantage of the light before the canopy closes, and then dying away until the following year. The flowers are a rich and glossy yellow, each surrounded by a ruff of backswept bracts, which gives them their country name of choirboys; on cold days, when the temperature remains below ten degrees, the petals remain shut up into little globes, as though each bud were the golden centre of a green daisy.

Dorothy L. Sayers often recalled her arrival as a small child at Bluntisham Rectory in Cambridgeshire, which was to be the family's new home. 'It was January, and the winter must have been mild that year, for the drive near the gate was already bright yellow with winter aconites – a plant which is said never to grow except where the soil has been watered by Roman blood,' she wrote in her 1952 Address to the Association for Latin Teaching. 'For all I know, this is true; for they grow thickly in my present garden in Essex, which lies along the road by which the emperor Claudius marched upon Colchester.'

Winter aconites are not native to the UK and were first recorded as naturalised in 1838. Hailing from south-east France, Italy and the Balkans, it's likely that their distribution reflects their geographical and climatic origins, and preference for calcareous soils – but I prefer the Roman story, and reserve my right to propagate it just as Dorothy did.

29 February 2020

In the dull days after Storm Dennis a barn owl braved daylight and drizzle to go hunting, quartering the rough grass around the village playground before drifting to the churchyard where a summer's-worth of wildflowers have died back to leave excellent habitat for voles, shrews and mice. To fly at midday in the rain it must have been famished; no surprise, after weeks of terrible weather at a time of year when rodents are already less active and harder to catch. Unlike other raptors, owls' feathers aren't waterproof, the trade-off for their silent flight; unless they're desperate they avoid going out in the rain, as a sodden, cold owl can quickly die of hypothermia.

My friend Sophie texted to say she thought one might be roosting in her hay barn, and I hurried over. She was right, and we picked up several pellets under the crossbeam, on the bales. They were smaller than usual, each containing just one set of bones rather than the three or four that are proof of a decent night's hunt. With numbers down by about 70 per cent and only about four thousand pairs left in the UK, every barn owl is precious, and Sophie is determined to help protect hers.

An even greater danger than bad weather is traffic; about a third of the barn owls that fledge each year will be killed on motorways and dual carriageways. These magical birds float low and slow as they hunt verges and field margins, making them vulnerable to fast-moving traffic – particularly if a trunk road isn't screened with trees to force them to gain height. A further risk is mouse and rat poison; rodents can take days to die, during which time they are often predated. Recent government figures showed that 90 per cent of barn owl carcasses contained rodenticide.

Having evolved to take advantage of human structures – as swallows and swifts have, not to mention mice and rats – it seems unfair that barn owls are now losing suitable breeding sites as we convert barns into dwellings and make no provision for them to nest. Sophie's barn is large and dry with an open side for access, an ideal spot for the nest box she's bought from the Barn Owl Trust – especially if nearby areas of rough grass are left unmown to create enough small mammal habitat to feed any chicks.

'You want me to cut back those twigs at the front?' asked my elderly neighbour as, at his insistence, he helped me cart and stack a delivery of firewood. 'Is it in your way at all?' I realised he meant the wintersweet hedge that divides our front gardens; perhaps he had seen me getting out of my car into a profusion of flowers, and was worried I minded. 'God, no,' I replied; 'it's covered in bees!'

Chimonanthus praecox is a frost-resistant shrub from mountainous China that was first introduced here in 1766. It flowers from November to March on bare stems (*Chimonanthus* means 'winter-flowering') and its fragrance is irresistible to pollinators; there were honeybees on it towards the end of January, and bumblebees – thought to be undergoing a mass extinction – are visiting it daily now.

For the rest of the year wintersweet is quite nondescript, and given that it takes a few years to flower I can see why impatient gardeners might not bother with it. But there's not much out there for insects at the start of the year, so to me, a flowering, hardy shrub like wintersweet is worth its weight in gold.

Reading Philip Pullman's latest I was entranced by his evocation of 'the secret commonwealth': the realm of 'things unseen', peopled by a throng 'invisible to ordinary vision' – for that is what the natural world seemed to me when I was a child. Alongside our daily human dramas acted another cast of characters, just as important as we were; a company whose tragedies, triumphs and nocturnal revels were revealed by arcane signs. I borrowed an animal tracking book from the school library so often that I wasn't allowed it any more, but its pictures of footprints in mud and snow, droppings, burrows, nibbled hazelnuts and other clues to the secret commonwealth of wildlife never left my mind.

I'm no animal tracker now, but I am a decent noticer. I learned it not from a book, but from my dad, who died last month. Leading his six children on hikes across Dartmoor in all weathers, in search of stone rows or hut circles, he'd stop to examine everything from violet dor beetles to fox scat and map lichen, exhorting us to remember so we could consult an *Observer's* guide, or *The AA Book of the British Countryside*, when we got back. To him, being curious about the world was only natural. To us kids it has proved the greatest of gifts.

4 April 2020

I glimpsed it first through slatted blinds: a bird motionless against blue, its rich russet back lit by afternoon sun, small head still below working wings. A kestrel was hovering over the field at the back of my cottage, and I grabbed my binoculars and raced to an upstairs window for a better view.

I see kestrels more often than any other bird of prey, yet for me – and unlike buzzards, which are much less common in East Anglia – they have never lost their allure. Each encounter leaves me thrilled by the sheer charisma of these perfect, graceful little raptors. And they're brave too; not long ago I watched a female struggling to take off from a ditch beside a black-timbered Suffolk barn while carrying a wriggling, fully grown rat.

Until now, most of my kestrel sightings have been from the car. They hunch on telephone wires like slim, long-tailed pigeons, scanning the pasture below; they drop from roadside trees and skim away over stubble fields. One haunts an abandoned airfield not far from my cottage, a tiny, sleek replacement for the B-17s that once flew there.

I'm lucky enough to be able to walk from my cottage straight into open fields, but when I'm on foot they usually spot me long before I see them, and make off. So to see one while indoors was a treat, and I watched it for as long as I could and with an even greater intensity than usual, drinking in its wildness, hoping for a stoop.

It never came. With the nonchalance characteristic of kestrels it tipped out of its hover into a long, curved sweep and disappeared; 'then off, off forth on swing / As a skate's heel sweeps smooth on a bow-bend', as Gerard Manley Hopkins wrote in 'The Windhover', his reference to ice-skating perfect not just for its grace but also for the feeling that comes with it of excitement and adrenalin.

This time, in lockdown, the sighting was bittersweet. I returned to my desk, but not to my work. Cooped up and suddenly fretful, I couldn't help but picture the wide, empty, sunlit fields the kestrel was flying over, and its heedless and uninterrupted freedom of the skies.

Also on the wing now is a far humbler creature, the little ladybird. Warm weather brings them out of hibernation, and they spend the summer helpfully eating both adult and larval aphids on rose bushes, fruit trees, honeysuckle and other garden plants.

Few insects command such strength of positive feeling or have amassed so many nicknames over the centuries. Here in Suffolk a ladybird is a bushy bandy; elsewhere, they're goldie-birds, red-coats, ply-goldings, sodgers, cushy cows, clock-leddys, king alisons and dozens of other names. Welsh renders them as *buwch goch gota* (little red cow) or *Siân ffa* (Jane the bean). Children are drawn to their redness and pleasing roundness, and until recently most adults retained a positive feeling about them too. So it's a great shame that their reputation has been so damaged by their cousin the harlequin ladybird. This disease-resistant species arrived in 2004 and has spread rapidly across the UK, primarily by having several broods per year and not only outcompeting but actively predating our native ladybirds. Indoors they will consume wallpaper, curtains and carpets, and exude both a sticky black excreta and a foul-smelling liquid from their joints if squashed.

There are fifty-three native ladybirds in Britain, twenty-eight of which are the round, dotted types we're used to seeing; of those the seven-spotted and two-spotted remain the most common. All lack the white triangle that appears at the back of the harlequin's head. Surrey is, for mysterious reasons, a particular hotspot for Britain's ladybirds, something known to entomologists as the 'Molesey Phenomenon'.

Spring is unfurling its glory across city and countryside, with no regard for our locked-down lives. Chiffchaffs have flown in and are *dink-dink-dink*-ing from every copse and thicket, newly arrived blackcaps are adding a jubilant note to the swelling dawn and evening choruses, there are brimstone butterflies, primroses and tadpoles, and on a shady bank near my cottage the first, early cow parsley is coming out.

For some, spring is making confinement feel worse; but I find it immensely comforting to sense the seasons' ancient rhythm, altered but as yet uninterrupted, pulsing slow beneath our human lives. Suffolk's nightingales will return, and if none sing near enough for me to enjoy them this year, of course I'll be disappointed; but the natural world exists in spite of our requirements and our depredations, and it's in precisely this that lies its enduring strength. Onwards spring romps, as miraculous and dizzying as ever, whether humans are there to witness it or not.

9 May 2020

Suffolk's spinneys and copses are carpeted in wildflowers, and the fragrance is intoxicating. Some will doubtless be bluebell woods; but around my home wild garlic is king.

Ramsons crop up all over the place here, including in my garden, but there are two woods I can reach on foot where the broad, glossy straps of their leaves have been creating an unbroken emerald sea for weeks, and where now the white stars of their flowers glimmer among them, ethereal yet earthily pungent.

Woods such as these have long been landmarks, as evidenced by old place names: Ramsbottom, Ramsholt, Ramsey, Ramshope. Really dense colonies take a great many decades to establish, and ramsons en masse can act as a clue to the age of a wood.

And they're not the only white flower in perfection at the moment: May blossom is turning hedgerows into swags of cream, stitchwort embroiders the verges and cow parsley froths from roadsides, ditches and wood margins. One of several similar-looking plants once known as Queen Anne's lace (along with bishop's weed and wild carrot), cow parsley also has the unsettling old name of mother-die. Some white umbellifers, such as hemlock and giant hogweed (not the common sort), can be toxic, so perhaps the nickname was simply a good way of keeping country children from harm; however, it makes an excellent cut flower, and is common enough – increasing, in fact – to safely pick.

I may miss out on seeing sheets of wild bluebells this year, but I know how fortunate I am to be able to see anything of spring. My niece, who is high-risk, is isolating in a one-bed London flat with no garden; close friends are trying to keep a five-year-old healthy and stimulated while remaining almost entirely indoors. But others I know are finding huge solace and interest in their daily walks, no matter how unprepossessing their local area.

I think of Patrick Kavanagh's deep belief in parochialism, of the coach-sick Revd Gilbert White who rarely left his beloved parish, and Suffolk farmer Adrian Bell, *The Times*'s first crossword setter, who preferred walking, or a pony and trap, over the new fad of motorised transport: 'while the circumference of miles at one's disposal is halved, their content is more than doubled,' he wrote. We may not be able to go far at the moment, but many of us are noticing so much more.

Twice in recent days I've got up before sunrise and headed out to hear the dawn chorus, taking a field recorder so I can capture it for the podcast I'm making to keep people in lockdown in touch with the natural world. In towns and cities robins are often the first to give voice, often while the sky is still black; here in Suffolk it's been the job of the skylarks, hanging over the dim fields.

I was cheered to hear the notes of yellowhammers from the hedges, though I was confused by one, who sang 'A little bit of bread and no—' without the customary addition of 'cheese'. One of the few birds to sing right through to late summer, they soundtrack August strolls along hot country lanes and walks on sun-baked, gorse-clad uplands. Once they were known as scribble larks or writing larks for the intricate patterns on their eggs.

These grain-eating birds have been in steep decline across western Europe since 1980, and the issue seems to be one of winter survival. Once, they could feed on grain spilled on stubble fields in colder weather, as well as weed seeds from 'unimproved' hay meadows, but agricultural intensification has vastly reduced both stubble and weeds. Properly planned, consistent agri-environment schemes are vital if we are not to lose farmland birds like yellow-hammers from our countryside, and with them part of our shared cultural heritage: that age-old, deeply evocative song.

When your life's work is trying to connect people to nature, seeing so many newly tuning in to birdsong, revelling in rain showers and hungry for the rites of spring is deeply satisfying. Suddenly, it seems, there's space for the small, seasonal pleasures that sustain some of us, but which have gone unnoticed by many, stuck on the exhausting tread-mill of travel and shopping and work: the first swift, the heady scent of lilac, a blackbird's evening song.

If we could take one thing from this nightmarish period and carry it into whatever world is to come, I'd choose this fragile new awareness, this new need for nature, this sudden new love. It contains everything we need in order to transform the way we live, individually and collect-ively – if we can only nurture it. This could be the start of something wonderful.

13 June 2020

At last the endless, sun-drenched spring is over, and summer is coming in. Hawthorn blossom and cow parsley have handed over to ox-eye daisies and dog roses in

Suffolk's hedgerows, the oilseed rape is no longer yellow, and – held back a little by the long dry spell – the wheat and barley are now over knee height.

Young wheat, before it ripens, has a bluish cast; it stands stiff and unmoving in the fields, a uniform foil to the stripes of crimson poppies at the margins. Barley, in contrast, is a softer apple green, and ripples with even the lightest breeze.

Around my village the wild roses are spectacular. Where hedgerows haven't been flailed to within an inch of their lives they're garlanded with pink and white dog roses held on slim, arching stems. There are field roses, too (*R. arvensis*), similar to their cousins but with pure white blooms, and sweetbriars, or eglantines (*R. rubiginosa*), which are rosier than even the pink dog roses.

These are humble flowers in comparison to the lavish cultivated roses I've been looking at for my garden, yet their simple beauty seems perfectly to suit the tangled June hedgerows with their noisy cargoes of fledgling birds. And later in the year – unless the tractor comes around with its cutter bar – there'll be the red hips we used to make itching powder from, and which are a vital food source for overwintering birds.

The ox-eye daisies, too, are lovely in their simplicity, their white petals arranged around a yellow centre like a child's drawing. But in fact what we think of as petals are ray flowers, their long, white ligules extending outwards and helping to direct insects to the central collection of tiny yellow disc flowers, where the pollen, stamen and pistils can be found.

I still associate ox-eyes with *The AA Book of the British Countryside*, which featured them on its wraparound cover. A staple of many homes in the 1970s and 1980s, I pored over it obsessively, reading about everything from agricultural methods to rare orchids, vernacular architecture to rock pools and woodland ecosystems to the Countryside Code. The sense it gave was of a stable, undisputed body of knowledge that could easily be transferred to a willing reader. In today's more complex and pluralised world, such certainty is harder to find.

Each year I try to learn at least one new bird's song, and this year, thanks to a *Times* reader, it's been the lesser whitethroat. Last month I wrote about a yellowhammer with a slightly unusual song, and Stephen Bueno de Mesquita posted a comment online suggesting a possible culprit. He was right, and I'm so pleased to add another species to my repertoire, and to feel that the fields around me have got a little richer for knowing that this shy little migrant is about.

Unsurprisingly, given his excellent track record in taxonomy, it was the parson-naturalist Gilbert White who first identified the lesser whitethroat in this country. 'An uncommon, & I think a new little bird frequents my garden,' he wrote in *The Natural History and Antiquities of Selborne*, published in 1788. 'It much resembles the white

throat, but has a more white, or rather silvery breast &
belly; is restless & active like the willow-wrens, hopping
from bough to bough, & examining every part for food. It
also runs up the stems of the crown-imperials, & putting
its head into the bells of those flowers, sips the liquor contained in the nectarium of each petal. It sometimes feeds
like the hedge-sparrow, hopping about on the grass-plots
& mown walks.'

Although I now hear lesser whitethroats on nearly every
walk, I still haven't spotted one. Churlishly, bird guides
tend to describe their shy behaviour as 'skulking', in contrast to White's description; I suspect, though, that he was
both a more skilled and more patient observer than many
of us today.

My dog, Scout, was in London when lockdown hit, and
so has remained at her city residence rather than visiting her rural retreat. I miss her terribly, so have invented
another reason – making a weekly nature podcast – to
make sure I get out for a tramp around the woods and
fields each day.

I've walked miles to record nightingales, paddled in a
river surrounded by damselflies, explored a ruined cottage
in the woods, watched a barn owl hunting, been dive-
bombed by swifts, cycled around in pursuit of a cuckoo,
stumbled on bell-ringers practising with handbells, got up
before 4 a.m. to record the dawn chorus, and have spent
this week trying to locate the sadly elusive purr of a turtle

dove. Any joy the podcast has brought listeners has been far, far outstripped by my pleasure in making it. Thank you to everyone who has so far tuned in.

18 July 2020

Returning to London after four locked-down months in rural Suffolk, I didn't expect a welcoming party – but what greeted me in the skies couldn't have gladdened my heart more had it been a sky-writer daubing my name on the blue. Standing on the balcony of the flat I'd borrowed from a friend I heard the cry of a bird of prey and glanced up to see not one, but two peregrine falcons circling high over the Barbican Estate, calling almost continuously to one another. Dumbstruck and dazzled, cursing my failure to bring my binoculars to town, I watched their joyful display for ten minutes until at last, harried by a lone gull, they disappeared from view.

A century ago, peregrines were extremely rare winter visitors to the capital; nowadays there are close to thirty territorial pairs, and they can be seen nesting everywhere from Tate Modern to Charing Cross Hospital, Westminster Abbey to the Houses of Parliament. This recent urban colonisation relates, in part, to their slow recovery from the population crash of the 1950s to 1970s, which affected all our birds of prey as a result of organophosphates in pesticides such as DDT. These increased in concentration as they passed up the food chain, resulting in catastrophic toxicity in apex predators; the shells of affected birds' eggs became so thin that few broods survived. But city peregrines are also taking advantage of both the rise in feral pigeon numbers and our use of street lights, which evidence shows is allowing them to hunt at night; it's also thought that a bird raised in the city will be more likely to choose an urban environment to nest in themselves, resulting in a modest exponential rise.

As I quickly discovered, right now there are two adult peregrines and at least three juveniles hunting the skies over EC2Y, the first time chicks have fledged here since 2016. Over the course of the weekend their fast, stocky silhouettes became a familiar sight – as did the remains of their kills, one pair of pigeon wings proving particularly attractive to a hulking herring gull who could barely be persuaded to step away long enough for me to take a photograph.

What a perfect location for these breathtaking birds of prey: tall, highly secure buildings for their eyrie, and a plentiful supply of the kind of prey we're happy for them to eat. It's so cheering when we manage to allow nature to thrive in our cities. I only wish the peregrines' recent story wasn't an exception, but the rule.

I returned to Suffolk with a head full of falcons, a much-needed haircut and the beloved dog I hadn't seen in four months. Out on a warm, drizzly walk the next day I found the wheat had turned golden in my absence, and the barley was fast losing the last of its pale green tint.

I walked a little further than I usually do, keen to show Scout the new routes I'd discovered in lockdown, and to make sure her first country walk in months was a good one. Turning for home at last, near a farm on the far side of the next village, I took a newly surfaced track through pea fields on which scarecrows stood sentinel dressed in motley collections of worn-out hi-vis.

And that's when I noticed what I was walking on: not just rubble and hardcore, but smashed white sanitaryware and, I realised with growing disquiet, truckloads of plastic: there were sun-bleached toys, broken toothbrush handles, flattened plant pots and all sorts of recognisable household waste.

I spend a good part of my life picking up litter, returning from walks with pockets stuffed with flattened drinks bottles, sweet wrappers, baler twine, downed helium balloons and – in a new and worrying development – blue PPE gloves. To discover that all the while plastic is being deliberately spread on to farmland by the truckload feels extremely dispiriting.

A looming book deadline has meant I've been spending every afternoon indoors, staring through blinds at my side return with its three wheelie bins. Happily, the narrow path is thronged with juvenile sparrows at the moment, who thrum around clumsily on brand-new wings, while on sunny days, next door's hebe has been covered in red admirals, peacocks, large whites and comma butterflies.

The warm, dry spring meant many species were seen on the wing earlier than usual this year, and coupled with the fact that the last two summers have been good for them, it's thought that 2020 could see a butterfly boom, with the possibility that some will be able to produce several broods – depending on autumn's weather.

It'll be interesting to see the numbers: this weekend it's the annual Big Butterfly Count, when people all over the UK will spend fifteen minutes counting butterflies and recording them either via an app or online. Go to bigbutterflycount.butterfly-conservation.org/ to take part.

22 August 2020

A blazing August afternoon, the bare ground dry and baking hot, thunderclouds massing on the horizon. Stuck at my desk, work not going well, I'd forced myself out of the house and was walking across a stubble field with my hands in the pockets of my dress and my head down, ruminating. Without warning, my heart jumped and began to pound, and all the hairs on my arms stood on end. Looking around for the source of this odd sudden fear, I saw a vortex of dust and straw about as tall as a man approaching silently from the left, at about running pace. It passed in front of me perhaps six feet away, meandered for thirty paces, slowed, and simply vanished, leaving no evidence of itself behind.

In America they're known as 'dust devils', in Egypt

they're 'fasset el 'afreet' (ghost winds) and in Australia 'willy-willys'; in Britain they were once called 'straw devils' for their habit of disarranging windrows of hay and tossing straw about. Here in Suffolk, for some reason, they were given the name 'Roger': 'We never dared leave door or windows open on the farm when haymaking as Roger [might] dump a pile of hay in the kitchen,' one Twitter correspondent told me. In Ireland, if a 'fairy wind' approached you'd cast a handful of whatever you were working on into the vortex as a form of propitiation, an impulse I can understand: despite recognising what it was, the phenomenon still felt extremely uncanny, its passage across the field completely unrelated to the prevailing breeze and strongly suggesting not the circular motion of heated particles but some kind of conscious intent.

Dust devils – which also occur on Mars – are electrically charged and create oscillating magnetic fields, and I won-der if that might explain my body's strange, preconscious hyper-alertness, seconds before one crossed my path. Cer-tainly, they appear in the folklore of many countries as supernatural beings intent on mischief, and in some cultures as positively evil. What it felt like to me was a haunting: an unquiet spirit tied to that one particular field that woke, and rose, and stumbled about in the daylight; and then was vanquished, and slipped back into the soil to sleep.

I'd thought the swifts had all flown south, but a neigh-bour appeared on my doorstep with closed hands and the dazzled facial expression that means someone is either newly in love or holding something feathered and other-worldly. It was a young swift, about three weeks old and not yet ready to fly, which had probably been blown out of its nest during a storm the night before.

Unlike most fledgling birds, this swiftlet was neither helpless, nor ugly, nor cute. Although *Apus apus* means 'footless', they do have feet, and this one clung to my fingers with strong little claws and tried to bury itself in my T-shirt. Folded, its wings reached about to its tail and had not yet developed into the extraordinarily long scimitars it would need in order not only to fly to Africa but to remain aloft for what could be several years. Yet its sleek head, with tiny beak and recessed eyes, already had all the gravity of a terrible angel brought to ground.

I drove it to my nearest volunteer swift rescuers, who pronounced it in good health and will feed it waxworms until it's ready to be released. They were looking after an unusual number of juveniles for this time of year, and it's not clear why some birds bred so late in the season. If you find a downed swift, don't launch it into the air or out of a window. Hold it up on a flat palm, but if it doesn't fly, search for details of your nearest swift rescuer online.

Suffolk is one of the UK's driest counties, and while the warm, fine spring made lockdown more bearable for those of us able to get outdoors, the prolonged lack of rain was bad news for farmers. Cereal yields have been low, and in some cases loss-making – though the hot weather meant that at least the harvest came in quickly, and in most cases without the need for the grain to be dried.

When the dry spell broke it broke over fields razed to stubble, drawing from them a quick green aftermath of wildflowers and agricultural 'volunteers': potato seedlings in the rape fields, stray sugar beet where the wheat was, a single broad blade of maize emerging like a flag from between the barley rows.

Already the stubble is being ploughed, the earth turned under and harrowed to a tilth, ready to be drilled again. The crops that were planted last autumn, when I moved to this village – and which I watched grow, change colour and ripen through months of lockdown – have now been gathered in. A brief moment to breathe, and gather our thoughts; and then the cycle starts again.

The Stubborn Light of Things *podcast*

A Guardian and Financial Times Podcast of the Year

Shortlisted for UK Podcast of the Year at the BPG Awards 2021

The critically acclaimed companion podcast to *The Stubborn Light of Things* finds Melissa Harrison exploring Suffolk's beautiful open countryside, documenting the wonder and richness of the natural world in intimate detail. Alongside extracts from her nature diary, the podcast features guest spots from the likes of Jini Reddy, Kathleen Jamie, Will Burns and Kate Bradbury, and snippets from the diaries of Gilbert White, England's most famous naturalist, charting our connection to the outside world, the weather and the changing seasons.

'Melissa Harrison's beautifully produced show takes us from this spring through summer into autumn . . . it's the atmosphere you get addicted to, the sounds and dreaminess, Harrison's close-up voice . . . gorgeous.' Miranda Sawyer, *Observer*

'The sense of pleasure, and the security that [Harrison] gets from her daily interactions with her surroundings, is audible . . . earnestly reflective . . . [its] crackling, windswept atmosphere is crucial to its charm.' Anna Leszkiewicz, *New Statesman*

www.melissaharrison.co.uk/podcast
Produced by Peter Rogers

Rain: Four Walks in English Weather

Longlisted for the Wainwright Prize

Whenever rain falls, our countryside changes. Fields, farms, hills and hedgerows appear altered, the wildlife behaves differently, and over time the terrain itself is transformed.

In *Rain*, acclaimed novelist and nature writer Melissa Harrison follows the course of four rain showers, in four seasons, across Wicken Fen, Shropshire, the Darent Valley and Dartmoor. Blending these expeditions with reading, research and memory, she reveals how rain is not just an essential element of the world around us, but a key part of the English identity too.

'[Harrison] has both the specialist knowledge and knack of language to explain why water falling from the sky is such a pleasurable part of daily existence.' Kathryn Hughes, *Guardian*

'One of the pleasures of Harrison's writing is that you need not be in the country for her powers of inspection, precise and delicate, to take effect.' Shahidha Bari, *Financial Times*

'[Harrison is] a refreshingly measured companion with a quick eye for the details.' Horatio Clare, *Daily Telegraph*

'Wonderful.' James Rebanks, author of *A Shepherd's Life* and *English Pastoral*

'A beautiful little book.' Philip Marsden, author of *Rising Ground*

faber

Sign up for free

Become a Faber Member and discover the best in the arts and literature

Sign up to the Faber Members programme and enjoy specially curated events, tailored discounts and exclusive previews of our forthcoming publications from the best novelists, poets, playwrights, thinkers, musicians and artists.

Join Faber Members for free at faber.co.uk

faber
members